Safe at Work?
Library Security
and Safety Issues

Teri R. Switzer

The Scarecrow Press, Inc.
Lanham, Maryland, and London
1999

SCARECROW PRESS, INC.

Published in the United States of America
by Scarecrow Press, Inc.
4720 Boston Way
Lanham, Maryland 20706

4 Pleydell Gardens, Folkestone
Kent CT20 2DN, England

Copyright © 1999 by Teri R. Switzer

British Library Cataloguing in Publication Information Available

Library of Congress Cataloging-in-Publication Data

Switzer, Teri R.
    Safe at work? : library security and safety issues / Teri R. Switzer.
        p.   cm.
    Includes index.
    ISBN 0–8108–3623–8 (alk. paper)
     1. Libraries—United States—Safety measures—Bibliography.
    2. Libraries—Security measures—United States—Bibliography.
    I. Title.
    Z679.7.S95   1999
    025.8'2—dc21
                                 98–50278
                                    CIP

♾™ The paper used in this publication meets the minimum requirements of American National Standard for Information Sciences—Permanence of Paper for Printed Library Materials, ANSI/NISO Z39.48–1992.
Manufactured in the United States of America.

This book is dedicated to my wonderful family — husband Gene Luthman, daughter Lois, son Vince — and to Jennifer Kutzik and other breast cancer survivors.

CONTENTS

INTRODUCTION

Library security covers a myriad of issues. The most common issues are the security of the collection and the safety of staff and patrons; however, it also includes disaster preparedness, preservation and conservation of materials, wellness issues for staff, and building design.

Issues of library security have been around for as long as libraries have been in existence. But, only recently have librarians been concerned with the whole realm of library security. The security-related issues of libraries mimic those of any other business or organization. Theft (by employees as well as patrons), violence, sexual harassment, and wellness issues such as ergonomics, stress, and indoor air quality are ever present in libraries, as well as retail businesses or other professional offices. Workplace crimes have increased dramatically during the past twenty years, and libraries have become popular victims of crime.

This annotated bibliography is devoted to the many facets of security and safety that are found in libraries. It is divided into eight chapters: security and safety issues, wellness issues, collection security, computer and technology issues, premise security, disaster preparedness, legal liability, and resources. Chapter one, "Safety and Security Issues," covers journal articles and monographs about general security issues such as workplace violence and problem patrons. "Wellness Issues," found in chapter two, cover a whole realm of topics that pertain to personal safety such as ergonomics, stress, and indoor air quality. Indoor air quality is a topic that is being discussed more frequently in libraries, but little library-specific literature is available. The last chapter, "Resources," is a potpourri of information: theses and dissertations, videos, alternative media, conferences, web sites, and serials. The majority of the references in chapter eight are from the private sector. Even though these references are not solely about libraries, libraries are businesses and most are run as businesses; therefore, many of the issues and the solutions are the same. In all, the citations are very selective but are representative of the literature found on these topics.

In preparing this bibliography, several paper, electronic, and Internet indexes were consulted: CARL's UNCOVER, *ABI Inform,* *Expanded Academic Index,* OCLC's *First Search, Psychology Index,* MEDLINE, PAIS, *Index to Library Literature, Library and Information Science Abstracts,* and *Electric Library.* Although there are several references to citations from Canadian, British, and Western Europe literature, the majority of the citations have been selected to ensure coverage of all aspects of library security in the United States. In general, only those articles and monographs of a substantive nature or those that illustrate a unique aspect of security and safety are included.

This bibliography could not have been completed without the valuable assistance of the staff and the student assistants in Interlibrary Loan at Colorado State University. At the start of my research, a devastating flash flood swept through the campus and destroyed more than 450,000 volumes of books and serials. Within days of the disaster, our Interlibrary Loan was up and running, writing computer programs to allow patrons to request and receive loan requests. Their creativity, coupled with the cooperation of regional libraries, has made it possible for researchers to continue accessing the literature needed.

1. SECURITY AND SAFETY ISSUES

In the not too distant past, the most common crime that beset libraries has consisted of vandalism and thefts of library materials. However, as the populace becomes more stressed-out and intolerant and as libraries begin to offer more services to their patrons, security and safety problems in libraries have increased. Great Britain's Education Service Advisory Committee of the Health and Safety Commission has taken a pro-active stance towards the safety of people working in educational environments. It says, "Ensuring health and safety in schools and colleges is an essential part of any school manager's responsibility. However, this cannot be achieved by one person. Overall effective health and safety management, including personal safety and security, has to be in place. It also has to reflect the more general aspects of management" (Lamplugh, 1996).

This philosophy is one that knows no boundaries, as it carries over from country to country, institution to institution, business to business. What are the problems that affect one's personal safety?

Libraries are no longer quiet places to read, research, or study. They are no longer refuges and places of solitude. Theft, drugs and alcohol, and violence against individuals such as rape and assault all plague those once quiet depositories of books. The social ills that plague one library may not be present in another, however, and these complex social problems are not the only issues that employees and patrons of libraries confront. There are also workers' compensation issues, such as those that arise due to repetitive motion injuries and hazards in the workplace that can cause physical harm.

Traditionally, libraries haven't spent much time on safety and security issues. Workplace violence, problem patrons, and sexual harassment are very important to today's library and its staff.

Workplace Violence

Violence has gone rampant, and violence in the workplace is increasing each year. In a twenty-year period, between 1971 and

1992, more than 36 million people were injured by violence (D'Addario, 1995). In addition, with the workforce spending 35-65% of their time at work, employees want to feel safe and free from threats (Capozzoli and McVey, 1996). No longer can organizations afford to ignore the possibility of workplace violence. There are several different methods or techniques promoted to defuse workplace violence. One of the more recently popular ones is zero-tolerance (Albrecht, 1997). There is no one program, however. Instead, organizations need to tailor-make their threat management plans to fit their own situations. Workplace violence can be either external or internal. Let's first look at internal forces, or violence caused by employees. There are several factors that an organization can employ to curtail employee violence. Some ideas include instituting a pre-employment screening process, establishing an employee assistance program, creating a threat management team, and developing a policy and procedure against employee violence (Puderbaugh, 1996).

A quick look at workplace violence shows that a person who is emotionally upset at work is two and a half times more likely to commit violence if he or she is using drugs or alcohol. Violence prevention can start with the initial employment interview — questioning who the individual is and looking at past violence since this is the single best predictor of future violence (Minor, 1995).

Pre-employment screening can be used as an important interview tool; however, its use can pose a dilemma for employers. Some state policies encourage rehabilitation and re-employment for ex-offenders. The use of pre-screening forms may conflict with these policies. In addition, Title VII of the Civil Rights Act of 1964 prohibits employment decisions based on an applicant's arrest record.

Another screening technique is the use of profiling for violent tendencies. The violent employee generally is:

- white male, twenty-five to forty years of age
- loner with a history of violence and a fascination with weapons
- socially withdrawn person with a history of interpersonal conflict, family problems and marital strife
- someone who often gives verbal expression to complaints about and to management, but then stops

- an angry person who has few outlets for that anger, but has requested some type of assistance in the past (DiLorenzo and Carroll, 1995).

However, profiling is not without potential liability. The Americans with Disabilities Act (ADA) offers protection for individuals with mental impairments. There have been occasions when an employee is discharged because he or she fits a profile of a person with violent tendencies and then files a lawsuit charging discrimination under the ADA. The Equal Employment Opportunity Commission (EEOC) offers guidelines for determining whether a worker poses a threat. A worker poses a threat if there is:

- significant risk of substantial harm
- risk specific to the individual
- risk specific to the current circumstances
- risk based on objective evidence (such as medical evidence)
- risk that cannot be reduced through reasonable accommodations, is it possible to reassign the individual to a different job or unit (DiLorenzo and Carroll, 1995).

Even though an organization may use pre-employment screening or profiling, it is still very possible that an employee will be hired who creates problems. In the event that an employee is found to be potentially violent or has started to exhibit violent behavior and management decides to discharge the employee, human resource managers need to take precautions during the discharging of the employee. Some tips on how to defuse anger during a termination include deal with the employee's feelings, provide information, focus on the future, summarize the major points, answer the employee's questions, and if appropriate, assign a liaison to monitor and stay in contact with the employee until the termination process is complete (Johnson, King, and Kurutz, 1996).

Problem Patrons

Problem patrons come in all ages, shapes, colors, and sizes, and both sexes. Some problems occur because patrons are upset about a fine or not finding the materials they need. Too often patrons become angry and disgruntled and take their anger out on the circulation or reference staff (Rubin, 1990).

Even though the typical problem patron is thought to be the angry irritable adult, many libraries, especially public libraries, find themselves with "latchkey" children. Libraries tend to be safe havens for children. It is common for children to drop by the library after school and wait until a parent can come. Many times, the children read books or participate in special library activities, but other times the children can become rowdy and disturb other patrons (Dowd, 1991).

To defuse potential or arising problems, staff need to know how to react. Most librarians are not mental health specialists; therefore, they should receive training on how to defuse tempers. A suggestion common throughout the security and safety literature is "have a policy." Dealing with problem patrons is no different. Policies outline the action to be taken and who is responsible for what.

One category of problem patron not included here is that of the homeless. Public libraries and public academic libraries are more susceptible to being frequented by the homeless. Libraries are warm and relatively safe, provide shelter and have rest rooms, couches, chairs, and tables. In addition, some have televisions with videos and listening rooms with cassettes and CDs, and all have computers, complete with Internet access. Generally speaking, though, the homeless are not security risks. If anything, they may be an annoyance due to offensive body odor. For that reason, caution should be followed when evicting a patron due to offensive body odor. Many states have statutes that protect libraries from problem patrons who truly are disruptive and interfere with the libraries' purposes; however, there is controversy over whether the homeless interfere with research and study simply due to poor hygiene (Davis, 1995). The Morristown, New Jersey, public library was brought into the public eye when a street person, Richard Kreimer, sued the library over its code of conduct that banned homeless people with poor hygiene from using their facilities (Hammeke, 1992). As more cities address library services to the homeless population, cases like this should become rare.

Sexual Harassment

Another safety issue in all workplaces is sexual harassment. Issues of sexual harassment are becoming more prevalent. Since the court case Meritor v. Vinson Savings Bank (477 U.S. 64, 1986), the climate surrounding sexual harassment in the workplace has become more secure; however, sexual harassment complaints are still occurring and need to be dealt with in a timely, professional, and non-threatening manner. It's important to remember that sexual harassment knows no boundaries and can affect both sexes (Rubenstein, 1992). Libraries always seem like the least likely place for security problems; however, unwanted sexual behavior can occur anywhere. What constitutes sexual harassment is a complex and confusing matter, and sometimes sexual harassment can be confused with an annoyance (Goodyear and Black, 1991). Regardless of which it is, any type of unwanted behavior can interfere with a person's ability to do his or her job and may have a negative effect on others. Even though there are several court cases involving sexual harassment, the overall anti-discrimination statute is Title VII of the Civil Rights Act of 1964, and sexual harassment constitutes sexual discrimination under the act. There are several steps that organizations should take to prevent sexual harassment from occurring.

- One of the first steps to sexual harassment prevention is educating staff. The chance that sexual harassment occurs is lessened if staff know the rules and what is acceptable behavior and what isn't.

- A policy and procedure delineating what should occur in the event a sexual harassment complaint is made can be beneficial to management and staff. The policy should state that the library does not tolerate sexual harassment on the part of anyone. It should also state what the procedures are when making a complaint.

- Disciplinary action should include a wide array of alternatives that range from a reprimand to dismissal, determined by the seriousness of the conduct.

- Supervisors need to know what their responsibilities are to their staff and to management.

- Library management needs to take all sexual harassment complaints seriously and conduct an investigation. An investigation can be productive in that it can clarify the issues and help management determine what went wrong and take measures to ensure a repeat won't occur.

- After an investigation is complete, a written report should be prepared that includes a summary of the allegations and the accused's response, a summary of who was interviewed, a presentation of the facts, and the recommendations (Gasaway, 1991).

All organizations have a responsibility to ensure a safe workplace. Sexual harassment is a violation of the law, and libraries need to be aware of their responsibilities and liability should a sexual harassment complaint be filed.

Summary

All one needs to do is take a quick look at an online catalog or even the World Wide Web to discover the vast amount of published literature on workplace violence, stress, ergonomics, sexual harassment, and problem patrons. The citations that follow are a very selective list of a small percentage of the literature written. Those listed are either more pertinent to the issues facing libraries or broad enough in scope that the information is notable.

Citations

General Safety Issues

Arterburn, Tom. "Librarians: Caretakers or Crime Fighters?" *American Libraries* 27 (August 1996): 32-34.

Libraries aren't only victims of crimes to materials, they also are victims of crimes to their staff and patrons. Northeastern University Library in Boston is reported to have the highest rate of personal property thefts of any other building on campus. Laptop computers are the most popular target for theft. Some security companies have developed a lock device to chain the personal computer to a table and lock the hard drive. Finding keys and locks too inconvenient, one library developed a security program that uses a fictional character holding stolen items and stationed it in the lobby to alert patrons about the hazards of leaving personal property unattended.

Barton, Laurence. *Crisis in Organizations: Managing and Communicating in the Heat of Chaos.* Cincinnati, OH: South-Western Publishing Company, 1993. 256pp.

The value and relevance of this book to workplace security are the appendices. Covered in the appendices is such information as the role of the Federal Emergency Management Agency (FEMA) in preparing for a crisis and a simple crisis management plan. There is also a very lengthy bibliography of books and articles spanning subjects such as environmental crises, sabotage, terrorism, and natural disasters.

Billings, Carol D. "Rights and Obligations of a Librarian." *LLA Bulletin* 59 (Winter 1996): 128-134.

This publication is the feature article for this issue, and it is one of insight about the dangers of being a librarian in Louisiana.

Bingham, Karen Havill. *Building Security and Personal Safety, SPEC Kit 150.* Washington, DC: Association of Research Libraries, 1989. 141 pp.

Bingham has compiled a representative sample of security documents, security position descriptions, policies on building security and problem behavior, and emergency procedures of 75% of the members in the Association of Research Libraries. Anyone wanting to revise or write a security policy should consult this kit first.

Bologna, Jack and Paul Shaw. *Corporate Crime Investigation.* Newton, MA: Butterworth-Heinemann, 1997. 250pp.

Employee theft, fraud, and embezzlement are potential problems in all organizations. This book is an excellent source of the procedures needed when one suspects an employee of a crime. Although libraries typically don't deal with large amounts of money, there is still the temptation to doctor overdue and lost-book fine payments, and even payments to vendors for acquisitions. The authors give a thorough examination of financial crimes law, how to detect embezzlement, and internal controls and safeguards to prevent and detect fraud.

Brady, Eileen E. *Library/Archive/Museum Security: A Bibliography.* Moscow, ID: Catula Pinguis Press, 1995. 64pp.

Although not annotated, this bibliography is a good representation of the literature published on library/archive/museum security. Articles, books, and audio-visual formats are covered, with the majority published in the 1980s and early 1990s. If using this source as part of a literature search, be careful because many of the citations are incomplete.

Brand, Marvin. "Security of Academic Library Buildings." *Library and Archival Security* 3 (Spring 1980): 39-47.

The University of Houston Libraries is the source for the material in this article. Brand, well known in the library security world, has compiled a checklist for physical and operational library security.

— — — . *Security for Libraries: People, Buildings, Collections.* Chicago, IL: American Library Association, 1984. 120pp.

Until recently, libraries didn't spend much time on safety and security. This book gives excellent historical coverage of security issues in libraries. In the fourteen years since it was written, security and safety has been addressed in most libraries; however, it is interesting to read about the security practices and concerns that were prevalent in the early 1980s.

Burns Security Institute. *National Survey on Library Security.* Briarcliff Manor, NY: Burns Security Institute, 1973. 38pp.

Yes, this is twenty-five years old, but it is an excellent source of historical statistics. It can also serve as a sad reminder that even though libraries have security systems, materials are still being stolen at rates as high as they were in the early 1970s. It's interesting to note that violent crimes are up from 1973. A copy of the survey that was sent to the 255 libraries is included, along with the number and kinds of responses.

Chadley, Otis A. "Campus Crime and Personal Safety in Libraries." *College & Research Libraries* 57 (July 1996): 385-390.

Campus crime is increasing so much that in 1992, Congress passed the Crime Awareness and Campus Security Act that requires campuses to report the crime rate and types of offenses occurring on campus. Even though campus crimes are not new, they are increasing and academic libraries are very vulnerable to violence. Most campus libraries have open-access policies that allow anyone to enter and use the collection. Academic libraries are also open nights and weekends. In addition, campus libraries are usually separate from other buildings and are more isolated. Because of these vulnerabilities, academic libraries need to take measures to protect themselves from crime. First, a security audit or checklist ought to be in place to help define the vulnerabilities, then steps need to be taken to make the library safer. Consider placing emergency telephones on each floor, giving patrons and staff whistles, and using security officers to patrol the stacks. Make sure the outside and perimeter is well lighted and make sure staff are trained in crime prevention.

Chaney, Michael and Alan G. MacDougall. *Security and Crime Prevention in Libraries.* Aldershot, England: Ashgate, 1992. 307pp.

Chaney and MacDougall have compiled a very informative book that covers physical and personal crimes in libraries. These two broad headings are broken down into smaller issues such as copyrights, insurance implications, security policy formulation, and book detection systems. The premise that overshadows each chapter is the same — crime in libraries does exist, in spite of the seemingly cloistered atmosphere. Even though this book has a definite British slant, the information that is given knows no boundaries. One of the more unique chapters is by Harry Faulkner-Brown on the role of architecture in security of buildings. Eight case studies dating from 1963 to 1982 are given, with each showing an example of the close relationship the architect and the librarian had in designing buildings.

Chartrand, Robert Lee. "Libraries in Perilous Times: Responsibilities and Opportunities." *Special Libraries* 78 (Spring 1987): 73-85.

Emergency preparedness is an important responsibility for library management. As important as being prepared to handle an emergency is the ability to manage information systems. These information systems include those for collecting, storing, and retrieving data. As storage facilities of documents, libraries have a responsibility to the community to provide information that could be used by emergency planners. Maps, architectural drawings, and federal and state documents may need to be made available to emergency planners.

Chilcoat, Jennifer E. "Creating A Safer Workplace — Personal Safety Considerations for Libraries." *Arkansas Libraries* 50 (October 1993): 18-20.

Recognizing that a business' greatest asset is its people, the author gives tips on keeping library staff and patrons safe and secure. Chilcoat states that security measures fall into two categories — staff preparedness and physical facility considerations. Under staff preparedness are considerations to undertake when establishing emergency communications protocol: try to schedule two or more people to work together if stationed in an isolated area of the building, train staff to handle problem patrons, and hire a security guard. Libraries also need to look at the building. Make sure all areas well lighted, limit access to bathrooms and other isolated areas, create barriers in the event an employee is confronted by a violent patron, provide more than one escape route, establish good relations with law enforcement, install security cameras, and install silent alarms or "panic buttons."

Clark, James H. "Making Our Buildings Safe: Security Management and Equipment Issues." *Library Administration & Management* 11 (Spring 1997): 157-161.

Three components of security should be addressed when drafting a security plan: the physical security of the building; the operating procedures for library staff, the public, and security personnel; and the security force that works in the building. Clark examines these three components and offers suggestions on incorporating each into the general security of library buildings.

Clementi, Gregory L. "A Secure Library Is a Blend of Technology and Cooperation." *Campus Law Enforcement Journal* 17 (July/August 1987): 6-11.

A Youngstown, Ohio, police officer, Clementi has written this article with a definite police professional's view in mind. It is authoritative and informative. Although the article could have a more definite library perspective, it is still very good and reinforces the need for active communication between the police department and library management.

Covington, Louis. "Safety Measures for Small Public Libraries." *LLA Bulletin* 59 (Winter 1996): 126-127.

Employers are responsible for providing a reasonably safe, psychologically secure work environment for their employees. After an incident at the Bossier Parish Library in Louisiana, the following steps were taken: every branch and department received a panic button, a second employee was hired for the last two hours of operation each day, each circulation desk was equipped with a can of Mace spray, additional exterior lighting was installed, dummy surveillance cameras were installed, and special code words were assigned to use when having to alert the library director or supervisory staff to call police.

"Crime Risk Revealed." *American Libraries* 11 (September 1980): 474.

This news article takes a glance at the damage and loss of books as a result of patrons/human sources. Reporting from a

Massachusetts survey, it is noted that more than 80% of the responding libraries reported that destruction to library materials was intentional.

Crimmin, Wilbur B. "Institutional, Personal, Collection, and Building Security Concerns." In *Security for Libraries: People, Buildings, Collections,* edited by Ruth Kaplan. Chicago: American Library Association, 1984. 24-50pp.

Crimmin discusses public library security issues in this article. Starting with the definition of security, he takes a step-by-step approach to guiding the reader through some of the security concerns. These include security of collections, the building, and the site/premises.

Crocker, Jane Lopes, Ellen Tiedrich, and William Bailey. "Security in the Smaller Academic Library." *New Jersey Libraries* 27 (Fall 1994): 6.

Most of the literature that discusses security in academic libraries focuses on the larger sized library. This article fills a void in the literature because it talks about the smaller sized academic library. Smaller academic libraries not only have fewer materials, but they also service a less populated area, the building is smaller in size, and the staff are few in number.

Cronin, Mary J. "A Workshop Approach To Library Security." *Library and Archival Security* 3 (Spring 1980): 49-56.

Training is especially important when keeping libraries and materials safe and secure; however, when this article was written, there were few training materials available. As a consolation to this problem, the library council of metropolitan Milwaukee, Wisconsin, developed a package workshop called "People, Problems, and Policy." The author describes the process that took place in planning and developing the training program. Don't let the date fool you, though, because the process that was used is timeless.

Currie, Susan. "Cornell University Libraries' Security Checklist." *Library & Archival Security* 7 (Summer 1985): 3-4.

Currie describes the checklist that Cornell University Libraries drafted. The checklist covers all aspects of library security and is an excellent model for other academic libraries to use.

Davis, Patricia J. "Libraries In Crisis: Safety and Security in Today's Library; or, I've Seen Fire and I've Seen Rain." *Texas Library Journal* 71 (Summer 1995): 90-93.

Libraries are becoming a catchall for a wide variety of patrons. Some use the library as a place to sleep, work, or change clothes in; others sit and talk loudly to invisible people. Are these people disturbing others and scaring off legitimate patrons? A library's mission is to serve the public and provide free access to materials. The security professional's mission is to keep the library safe and secure for its patrons. The two professions have to work together. Reporting on a workshop held by the Texas State Library, Davis' article focuses on tips and suggestions given by Warren Graham, head of security for the Charlotte and Mecklenburg County Public Library in North Carolina.

DiLorenzo, Louis P. and Darren Carroll. "Screening Applicants for a Safer Workplace." *HR Magazine* 40 (March 1995): 55.

Organizations not only have a moral and ethical duty to keep their employees safe but employers also need to be aware of liability issues. There are several theories why workplace violence has increased. These range from television, movies, and books to relaxed gun laws. Regardless of the reasons, organizations need to do something to counter-act the problem. One method organizations can use is to screen job applicants carefully. Computer technology has made it possible to check out the criminal histories of job applicants. However, this process is in conflict with some state policies, and it has been argued that the procedure conflicts with Title VII of the Civil Rights Act of 1964. Because this leads to a form of discrimination, employers need to be careful. Profiling programs can also run afoul of the Americans with Disabilities Act (ADA). For example, an applicant with a mental disability may be profiled as one with violent tendencies. Before using profiles as a screening tool, employers need to look at five questions: 1) is there a significant risk of a substantial degree, 2) is there a risk that is specific to an individual, 3) is there a risk that is current, 4) is the risk based on objective evidence, and 5) can reasonable accommodations be instituted to alleviate the risk.

Dougherty, Richard M. "Security in Libraries: User Groups and Physical Access." *Library Issues* 6 (July 1986): 1-2.

Knowing the library's users and what areas must be made available to them are two components of library security. Different libraries have different clientele, and knowing who comprises that clientele is important. In addition, considering physical access to the collection is also meaningful. Libraries exist to provide access to materials. However, it is important to take precautions in order to protect the collection.

Duitman, Patty. "Perils and Pitfalls in the Library." *Alki* 10 (December 1994): 16, 20.

Duitman relays some important advice on how to protect oneself from the various perils that befall library employees.

———. "Perils, Pits and Pitfalls in the Library." *PNLA Quarterly* 60 (Winter 1996): 11-12.

Libraries face the same security issues as other workplaces. Duitman comments on some of the safety issues in libraries. Computer security issues, ergonomics, and violence all plague American libraries. Duitman concludes that safety is everyone's responsibility and violence in the workplace is a social problem, not just a library problem.

———. "Staff Safety." *Alki* 11 (March 1995): 22.

Duitman emphasizes the importance of taking precautions when closing the library at night. She suggests these steps: do not walk through a dark parking lot alone, don't let a stranger walk you to your car, be aware of your surroundings, park in well-lighted areas, be alert when walking through a parking lot. Libraries should also take a pro-active stance and make sure all staff are trained in conflict resolution and handling emergency situations.

Elias, Marilyn. "Making Jobs Safe, Psychologists Aim to Keep Danger at Bay." *USA Today* (August 8, 1996): D1-2.

In 1994 there were 160,000 people physically assaulted and 1,071 murdered in the workplace. Because this figure is not predicted to decrease, defensive security measures are needed. Robbery-related violence could be deterred by locks, restricted access, and bullet-proof barriers. However, violence at the hands of an employee takes different measures. Managers need to learn how to defuse tempers before they explode.

Enssle, Halcyon. "Security Following a Disaster: The Experience at Colorado State University." *Colorado Libraries* 24 (Fall 1998): 16-18.

A flash flood that caused havoc and devastation at Colorado State University in July, 1997 also proved to be a real test for Colorado State University Libraries. Enssle takes a rather detailed look at what security issues were readily apparent and the steps the library took to remedy them.

Ettore, Barbara and Donald J. McNerney. "Human Resources: Managing Human Capital for the Future." *Management Review* 84 (June 1995): 56.

Human resource professionals have long been aware of the necessity of ensuring the safety of their employees. At the 1995 conference of the American Management Association, workplace violence was a theme of one of the panel discussions. The panel was comprised of Dale Masi of Masi Research Consultants; Mike Deblieux, president of Deblieux Human Resources; Boris Melnikoff, senior vice president and corporate director of security for Wachovia Corporation; and Michael Lowenbaum, a labor attorney from St. Louis, Missouri. Using personal experiences, the panel members discussed the rising incidents of workplace violence and what the human resource manager can do to prevent it. Some suggestions include banning weapons from the work site, enhance security around threatened individuals, encourage employees to be alert and report what they see, and train employees to know the warning signs of violent behavior. The value in reading this article is in the firsthand advice the panel members gave.

Fennelly, Laurence J. *Museum, Archive and Library Security.* Boston: Butterworth-Heinemann, 1983. 891pp.

This is a very complete book, with chapters written by twenty-two experts in the field of special situation security. It is a bit out of date, but most of it still provides valuable information relating to the security of collections.

Fields, Alison. "The Occupational Health and Safety Experience at Dunedin Public Libraries." *New Zealand Libraries* 48 (December 1995): 65-69.

In 1992 the Dunedin Public Library formed its Occupational Health and Safety Committee to "promote excellence in the management of health and safety in the Dunedin Public Libraries" and to ensure that accidents and hazards to staff and the public are minimized and to set up procedures for dealing with specific aspects of health and safety in the library. Fields explains the membership of the committee and outlines its functions and duties.

Fisher, Steven P. and Thomas K. Frey. "Security and Emergency Preparedness in a University Library: Planning Works." *Colorado Libraries* 23 (Spring 1997): 9-11.

Starting in 1992, the University of Denver library faculty took a good look at their security program and held several meetings to prioritize the issues and eventually come up with a disaster plan. Staff training is as important as the plan, and in order to make the plan work as it was intended, staff need to be trained in what to do in the event a security issue arises.

Flowers, Tom. "The Role of Maintenance in Promoting Safety and Health in Public Libraries." *Library Mosaics* 4 (July/August 1993): 20.

As maintenance manager of a New Jersey public library, Flowers recognizes the importance of being aware of potential hazards in maintaining the safety and well being of the library staff. Among some of the thoughts he gives is that it is important for all public institutions to investigate and follow procedures.

Gallagher, Stephanie. "Keep These Nine Digits to Yourself: Your Social Security Number Is Hardly Secure." *Kiplinger's Personal Finance Magazine* 51 (August 1997): 153-154.

Social security numbers are used for individual identification in dozens of transactions. Most libraries use them as identification numbers, as do banks, schools, and the government. Many of the databases that contain this information can be accessed online. Privacy experts warn that one's social security number is anything but safe, and they advise that social security cards are best left at home and personal documents that might contain social security numbers should be shredded.

Giacalone, Robert A. and Jerald Greenberg. *Antisocial Behavior in Organizations.* Thousand Oaks, CA: Sage Publications, 1997. 203pp.

Every employee is different, with some exhibiting attitudes and behaviors that are either not acceptable or have the potential of being harmful. The authors investigate issues such as employee revenge, aggression, lying, theft, and sabotage. Divided into chapters, with each written by specialists in the field, the information provided covers all aspects of anti-social behavior. Also included is a chapter on organizational culture and its relationship to anti-social behavior.

Griffen, Agnes M. "Potential Roles of the Public Library in the Local Emerging Management Program." *Special Libraries* 78(Spring 1987): 123-130.

Record and document storage of publications on disaster and emergency management and access to databases are functions libraries could perform to provide further order in case of an emergency. Community emergency response teams and public libraries can work in a cooperative nature to strengthen disaster preparedness measures.

Johnson, Dennis L., Christine A. King, and John G. Kurutz. "A Safe Termination Model for Supervisors." *HR Magazine* 41 (May 1996): 73.

It isn't a secret that a large percentage of violent workplace crimes are precipitated by the strong emotions from having been terminated. The authors report on a nine-step termination model suggested for use by managers and supervisors if they recognize signs that an employee has the potential to become violent. The nine-step model begins with identifying the problem behavior; determining if there are reasons for a progressive disciplinary action or if termination should be carried out; explaining the appeal procedures to the employee and monitoring the process; deciding whether to go ahead with the action, making plans for the termination interview; allowing for post-termination reflection; sharing the effects of the termination with the work group; and determining whether post-termination monitoring and counseling are appropriate. Throughout each step, six core responses are necessary: communicating, monitoring, documenting the organization's employee assistance program if there is one, knowing the organization's policies and procedures, and conducting self-reflection — how can you contribute to a safe and proper process?

Kamm, Sue. "A Rose is not Necessarily A Rose: Issues in Public Library Security." *Library & Archival Security* 13 (1995): 41-45.

Kamm used the experiences of the Inglewood, California, public library to illustrate the type of security problems that can be encountered on a daily basis in an urban public library. Shortly after Kamm wrote this article, the library contracted with a private security firm to patrol the building. Noting that vandalism is the most common problem, the author stresses the importance of erasing "tagging," or the intentional marking of property by gang members, as soon as they are noticed. It's also important to remember that vandalism can occur to materials, as well as to equipment and the building.

Keele, Herbert Charles. *Preventing Library Book Theft*. Suffolk, England: Access Keelaway, 1987. 88pp.

The first step in preventing the loss of library materials is to have an assessment of the library. What is the size and worth of the collection? Next, when a loss occurs, determine the size of the loss and note whether it is considered a significant loss. Keele starts with these questions and continues to probe into recognizing high-risk areas, security systems, staff training, and designing library layouts.

Keller, Daniel P. "University of Louisville Survey Finds Library Security Problems Becoming More Complex." *Campus Law Enforcement Journal* 17 (July/August 1987): 9.

This is a report of a 1985 survey that the University of Louisville (Kentucky) Campus Crime Prevention Program mailed to 1,410 college and university libraries in the United States. Nearly 27% of the libraries responded, and of those, one-half reported that theft of personal property was a serious concern, one-fourth were concerned for the personal safety of their staff, and nearly two-thirds did not report theft of library materials to campus security, even though 98% said they had had rare books and archival materials stolen. The value of this article lies in the overall attitude academic libraries have towards library security, even though they know they are being threatened.

King, Gary Thomas. "Preventing Personal Crimes." In *Is Your Library an Accessory to Crime?* Chicago: American Library Association, 1992. 3-6 pp.

King's article is a quick and to-the-point description of how libraries can prevent personal crimes from taking place in their buildings. He covers theft and assault and gives several tips on prevention measures for each crime.

Kirkpatrick, John. "Explaining Crime and Disorder in Libraries." *Library Trends* 33 (Summer 1984): 13-28.

This is a very good analysis of the sociological and psychological reasoning behind library crime, problems, and disruptive behavior.

Kirtley, Jane. "Shedding Light on Campus Crime." *American Journalism Review* 19 (July/August 1997): 50.

In 1974 the Family Educational Rights and Privacy Act was enacted to allow the sealing of files that identified all students, even those who had committed crimes. Coined as the "Buckley Amendment," the act was committed to stopping indiscriminate release of academic records. Over the years, however, schools have found that a downside to the amendment is that it prevents public access to campus security reports.

Kniffel, Leonard. "Facing Up To an Insecure Reality." *American Libraries* 27 (August 1996): 27.

This is a very realistic look at how crime is penetrating the hallowed walls of the American Library Association (ALA). What once used to be an organization with an atmosphere of congeniality and peace, the ALA headquarters now require identification badges, have guards posted at the entrance and patrolling halls, and have restricted building access hours. As editor of *American Libraries,* Kniffel states, "Libraries need rules of conduct. Learning from experience, courting threats with threats is the worst thing to do." He also asserts that denial is certain to take us farther from the ideal of how things should be — safe and sound.

Lamplugh, Diana and Barbara Pagan. *Personal Safety for Schools.* Brookfield, CT: Ashgate, 1996. 247pp.

Commissioned by the Suzy Lamplugh Trust, the national charity in England for personal safety, this book takes a hard look at the growing security problems in British schools, the responsibilities of administrators, and how the risks are reduced.

Layne, Stevan P. "Same Story . . . Different Day." *Library & Archival Security* 14 (1997): 45-51.

Prevention planning is a key phrase in the security protection world. However, policies simply stating what can or cannot happen are not sufficient. Layne takes a quick look at selecting alarm system vendors and selecting contractors for security and emergency planning. Even though it gives some good tips, the article has the distinct flavor of being an advertisement for the author's security consulting firm.

Lipinski, Barry V. "A Practical Approach to Library Security." *New Jersey Libraries* 27 (Fall 1994): 19-20.

Lipinski outlines practical advice libraries should take in order to keep their patrons and staff safe. Observe who enters and leaves the building, and investigate all instances when the exit alarm sounds.

Lincoln, Alan Jay. *Crime in the Library: A Study of Patterns, Impact, and Security.* New York: R.R. Bowker, 1984. 179pp.

Lincoln, known for his expertise in the library security field, has written a very informative book, albeit it is fifteen years old. Looking at public libraries, Lincoln uses tables to better illustrate his points. The statistics are staggering, and although they have improved, it is still recommended that libraries take precautions.

— — —. "Library Crime and Security: An International Perspective." *Library & Archival Security* 8 (Spring/Summer 1986): 1-163.

This publication should be called a single volume rather than an article because the entire issue is a treatise on library crime and security. Even though this article was written several years ago, the problems and the solutions are the same, we just need to learn from them. Libraries have problem patrons, vandalism, theft, and personal assaults. What makes this issue noteworthy is its international scope. British, Canadian, and United States library security concerns are described.

— — —. "Patterns and Costs of Crime." *Library Trends* 33 (Summer 1984): 69-76.

Lincoln presents a three-year study of crime in public libraries across the United States. Patterns of crime and security use are also covered.

— — —. "Patterns of Crime and Security in United States Public Libraries." *Library & Archival Security* 4 (1982): 1-11.

Lincoln gives the results of a survey sent to 406 public libraries in twelve eastern states on the incidence of crime.

— — —. "Protecting the Library." *Library Trends* 33 (Summer 1984): 3-11.

This article is actually the introduction to volume thirty-three of *Library Trends*, which is devoted solely to security issues in libraries. Lincoln's explanation for the rise in library crime is that incidents of crime have risen across the United States and crime in public places has increased as well. There are several risk factors inherent in libraries: most contain valuable, easily sold items such as books, CDs, artwork, and equipment, and most libraries are easily accessible to the public.

— — — and Carol Zall Lincoln. "The Impact of Crime in Public Libraries." *Library & Archival Security* 3 (Fall/Winter 1980): 125-137.

This article discusses crime that occurs in and against libraries. Also described are low-cost prevention programs such as the random presence of the police in the library, lock and key control, and an anti-vandalism public relations campaign.

Lizotte, Alan J. *Crime on Campus 1978-1979: A Survey of 150 College Campuses and Cities.* Ann Arbor, MI: Inter-University Consortium for Political and Social Research, 1985. n.p.(Data file)

This publication is an ERIC (Educational Resource Information Center) document, number ED286459. Included are statistics on violent crimes and property crimes. Even though the statistics are twenty years old, they are still daunting.

Lorenzen, Michael. "Security in the Public Libraries of Illinois." *Illinois Libraries* 79 (Winter 1997): 21-22.

Using data from a survey of Illinois public libraries, Lorenzen found that 58% noted that security was a problem and 26% reported that a staff member or a patron had been expelled or arrested during the past year. The statistics are not encouraging and illustrate the seriousness of security in today's library.

Maggio, Mark. "Keeping the Workplace Safe: A Challenge for Managers." *Federal Probation* 60 (March 1, 1996): 67.

Using the 1995 Oklahoma federal building bombing as its lead-in, this article takes an in-depth look at workplace safety and the responsibility of management to ensure employee safety. Today's workplace is ambiguous, uncertain, and tense. Reorganization and downsizing are just two of the problems plaguing managers and employees. As these and other issues surface, more people get pushed to their breaking points. However, co-worker violence that results in injury or death in the workplace is rather small. Instead, co-workers are more likely to be responsible for sexual harassment. The most obvious threats to employees come from customers or strangers. There are several steps that are available to management to ensure employee safety. One is to establish an employee assistance program; another is to establish a threat management team that aids in the education and training of employees.

Newman, John and Chris Wolf. "The Security Audit." *Colorado Libraries* 23 (Spring 1997): 19-21.

As more and more libraries become targets of theft, a formal security audit becomes more important as a prevention tool. Newman, a Colorado State University professor and archivist, and Wolf, a Colorado State University police officer, worked together to develop a security audit of the University Libraries Special Collections/University Archives. The four primary areas that were studied were the facility, the staff, the patrons, and the collection. Setting aside a two-hour block of time, the authors, the library security officer, and the risk management administrator met and began the arduous task of examining each security element. Some results of the audit were making adjustments to the false ceiling, increasing the fire alarm volume, instituting background checks for student staff and hourly personnel, and redesigning the book drop.

Nicewarner, Metta and Shelly Heaton. "Providing Security in an Urban Academic Library." *Library & Archival Security* 13 (1995): 9-19.

This article gives a general overview of the types of crimes in libraries, security measures, student security programs, expectations, and alternative solutions. Programs and experiences at the University of Nevada, Las Vegas library are related. Because the library is located in a high crime area, the authors' suggestions are valid and have been tested.

Powell, John W., Michael S. Pander, and Robert C. Nielsen. *Campus Security and Law Enforcement.* Boston: Butterworth-Heinemann, 1994. 289pp.

College and university campuses are, in reality, small communities and have the same types of safety and security problems. Even though this book covers all facets of campus security, there are a few that are of particular importance to a university or college library. Chapter twenty, "Protection of Special Campus Facilities," looks at the library, research facilities, and other facilities that require special security planning. Some ideas include installing book detection systems and an emergency alarm at the circulation desk that transmits a silent alarm to campus police, and controlling after-hours access to as few people as possible. In all, there are dozens of important ideas for library administrators and security officers detailed.

Quinsee, Anthony G. and Andrew C. McDonald. *Security in Academic and Research Libraries: Proceedings of Three Seminars Organised by SCONUL and the National Preservation Office.* Newcastle upon Tyne, England: University Library, 1991. 79 pp.

Divided into three parts covering security concerns of buildings, the collection, and employees, this book takes a complete look at security in libraries. The papers are from a series of three seminars given in the British Library on library security. Nearly every issue of library security is covered: legal processes, library building designs, and creating staff awareness.

Ragsdale, Kate W. and Janice Simpson. "Being on the Safe Side." *C&RL News* 56 (June 1996): 351-354.

Too often, emergency procedures don't take into account disabled patrons. This article details issues to cover and architectural considerations to keep in mind when looking at the safety of disabled library patrons.

Ramsay, John. "Safety in Small Libraries." *The Unabashed Librarian* 94 (1995): 5-6.

Prompted by a rash of violence in smaller public libraries, Ramsay notes these recommendations: have a second person on hand at all times, install an alarm that sounds directly at the police station, and discuss safety measures with the police department and come up with low-cost solutions to the safety problem.

Robertson, Guy. "Shelving and Safety: An Overview." *Feliciter* 42 (February 1996): 33-36.

Typically, librarians don't think of shelving as a potential security risk. Robertson examines different types of shelving and stresses the importance of conducting a risk analysis in order to address possible concerns before someone is injured.

— — —. "Unofficial Wisdom: A Review of Occupational Health and Safety." *Feliciter* 44 (March 1998): 14-19.

Robertson recognizes that across the nation, occupational health and safety committees are striving to protect libraries from a wide variety of risks. Workplace violence, fire hazards, and poor indoor air quality are only a few of the risks being addressed. In order to ensure that the committees are addressing the right issues and being productive, Robertson outlines twenty occupational health and safety issues to consider.

Rockman, Ilene F. "Coping with Library Incidents." *C&RL News* 7 (July/August 1995): 456-457.

Rockman takes a look at one model to use in training library staff to cope with crises. Six simulations are given that each staff member must comment on.

Savage, Noelle. "Facing Up to Library Security." *Wilson Library Bulletin* 58 (April 1984): 562-564.

Book theft and mutilation are growing problems, and to focus on these issues, the New York Metropolitan Reference and Research Library Agency sponsored a workshop on library security. The "fortification" suggestions are not, of course, unique or untried, but the primary importance of this article is that for years security measures have been suggested, but thefts and mutilation still take place. This must mean that one simply cannot read about security measures too often.

Shuman, Bruce A. "The Devious, the Distraught, and the Deranged." *Library & Archival Security* 14 (1997): 53-73.

No library is immune to threat, yet most crime that has occurred in libraries could have been deterred with careful planning and cooperation from staff. Shuman gives an in-depth view of security issues facing libraries today. Some issues to look at include problem patrons, building design, and security equipment. How far should a library go to reduce the likelihood that a criminal incident would occur? Is it necessary to install metal detectors? What areas should have limited access? Because there is no one correct way to prepare for every situation, Shuman gives a variety of scenarios to allow the reader to try a hand at solving the situation.

———. *Library Security and Safety Handbook: Prevention, Policies, and Procedures.* Chicago: American Library Association, 1998. 216pp.

Shuman's most recent monograph discusses the major risk factors libraries face today and offers strategies for writing security policies and procedures. Assessment tools used to identify risks are also included.

Smith, Michael Clay. *Coping with Crime on Campus.* New York: Macmillan, 1988. 246pp.

This is a twenty-eight-year look (1960-1988) at campus crime, the resulting legislation, and the number of court cases involving campuses. This book is good for a general, broad overview of the legal system as it pertains to college campuses.

Squibb, Molly, Rich Patton, and Linda Cumming. "Security Service with a Human Touch." *Colorado Libraries* 23 (Spring 1997): 6-8.

Some public libraries have the homeless as a security issue that most school libraries don't have. This article relates how the Denver Public Library extends its services to its homeless clientele and how it handles potential security problems with dignity.

St. Lifer, Evan. "How Safe Are Our Libraries?" *Library Journal* 119 (August 1994): 35-37.

Book theft and vandalism, security systems, and library budgets as impacted by crime are covered in this short article. St. Lifer offers some straightforward information about issues that have continued to plague libraries for many years.

Stambaugh, Sergeant Von I. "Fighting Crime through Prevention and Enforcement." *Campus Law Enforcement Journal* (July/August 1985): 15-16.

Theft, perversion, and destruction of materials are not uncommon in the college library setting. This article reports on the University of Toledo's (Ohio) stance towards curtailing thefts and educating potential victims. The university library's crime prevention program consists of a lecture for new students and parents informing them of potential problems and how to prevent these problems from occurring, posting flyers about specific problems, and educating library personnel to be alert to illegal activities in their areas. In addition, it is important that the library has a good working relationship with the campus police department.

Tehrani, Farideh. "Library Security." *New Jersey Libraries* 27 (Fall 1994): 4-22.

This issue of *New Jersey Libraries* is devoted to library security concerns. Some articles are cited in this bibliography, but for a well-rounded view of library security, check out the entire issue.

Thornton, Glenda A. "Guarding Against Chaos: Establishing and Maintaining Library Security." *Colorado Libraries* 23 (Spring 1997): 27-31.

After personally witnessing several people exit the University of Colorado-Denver Auraria Library through an emergency door, with no apparent alarm sounding, the author decided that security measures at the library needed to be studied and addressed. Both a financial audit and a security audit were conducted, but the results were not encouraging. Seven changes were made as a result of the audits, yet more work was needed. In all, the library underwent an extensive review and as a result the library now has a comprehensive security policy that works.

Turner, Anne M. *It Comes With the Territory: Handling Problem Situations in Libraries.* Jefferson, NC: McFarland, 1993. 197pp.

Turner has written an informative, practical book dealing with many of the key issues pertinent to library security. Chapters include tips on manual writing, staff training, and building security.

Tuttle, Judith A. "Security and Safety: University of Wisconsin-Madison Memorial Library Steps to Solve Problems." *Wisconsin Library Bulletin* 76 (May-June 1980): 135-144.

After having a patron attacked by an ax-wielding assailant, the University of Wisconsin-Madison Memorial Library decided to take measures to ensure patrons would be free from harm. The library administration worked with campus police, the dean of students, and campus women's groups to draft security measures. Among the measures instituted during the months following the discussions were the installation of both red emergency telephones and emergency exits so there is only one main entrance and one exit to the library building; the positioning of campus police in the building; and the introduction of the Whistle Stop Program that distributed whistles to patrons, and the drafting of press releases to the media about the new security measures implemented by the library.

United States Congress, Joint Committee on the Library. *Testimony on Library of Congress Security Proposals and Policies: Hearing Before the Joint Committee on the Library.* Washington, DC: Government Printing Office, 1994. 91pp.

This is the text of the testimony of Jim Billington's proposals regarding security in the Library of Congress. Even though the testimony is important and informative, one of the more valuable sections of the publication is the inclusion of the state statutes on theft and destruction of library materials, complete with the crime, the dollar amount of loss or damage, the maximum fine or imprisonment, and the statute citation.

Walch, T. "Improvement of Library Security." *College and Research Libraries* 38 (1977): 100-103.

This article investigates Walch's recommendations for improving library security. Many of them are not unique, but a few are ideas that could be overlooked. These are joining a registry service for lost or stolen archival materials and requiring a photo identification of all patrons.

Wensyel, James W. *Campus Public Safety and Security.* Springfield, IL: Charles C. Thomas, 1987. 204pp.

Chapter twelve is a must for campus library security officers to read, although scattered throughout the book are tips and tools for maintaining library security. Covered in chapter twelve are techniques to use to avert vandalism and theft of property and collections, fire and water damage, and damage from vermin. The author recognizes that many campuses don't just have one library building, but they also have departmental libraries located within a half-dozen or more buildings on campus. The advice varies from the practical (reduce the number of entrances and exits, and make sure the locks and hinges on the doors are sturdy) to the solid but impractical (no briefcases, and ask that folders and book volumes be left flat on tables and not leaning upright).

Williams, Wilda A. "A Prescription for Prevention." *Library Journal* 119 (August 1994): 38.

In this short article, Williams summarizes the 1994 ALA preconference, "Violence in the Library: Protecting Staff and Patrons." Presented as a panel discussion, this pre-conference provided excellent coverage of topics that are starting to plague more libraries — those of workplace violence, crisis management, security equipment, and building design. An overriding theme was to take precautions but don't install metal detectors. Instead, consider other devices such as duress alarms. Liability was also discussed, and it is generally held that libraries are not liable for acts of violence by patrons or employees unless it was foreseeable that such acts might occur.

Yarborough, Mary Helen. "Securing the American Workplace." *HR Focus* 71 (September 1994): 1-5.

This article cites statistics compiled by the foremost workplace security authority in the United States, Joseph Kinney. In a one-year period, July 1992 through July 1993, two million workers were physically attacked, six million were threatened, and another one thousand were killed. Coupled with these high numbers is an even higher figure associated with the cost of workplace violence. Some characteristics of at-risk work environments are chronic labor/management disputes, frequent grievances, an extraordinary number of injury claims, and an authoritarian management approach.

Young, Terrence E. Jr. "How Safe Are Schools? A School Librarian's Perspective." *LLA Bulletin* 59 (Winter 1996): 141-146.

As a librarian in the Jefferson Parish (Louisiana) public school system, Young knows firsthand about the issues facing school librarians, and security/safety is one of them. Young describes the national education goals that the nation's governors and the president drafted to address issues of school safety.

Workplace Violence

Ader, Elizabeth. "Violence in the Workplace: An Issue for Librarians." *Show-Me Libraries* 46 (Fall 1995): 12-14.

Librarians no longer can afford to ignore the potential risks associated with working in a library. Too often librarians work alone at night, exchange money with the public, work in high-crime areas, and are responsible for guarding valuable property or possessions. Librarians need to acquaint themselves with federal, state and local laws on illegal behaviors, know what can and cannot be done when confronting a threatening person, and check references carefully when hiring staff.

"Agencies Study Workplace Violence." *Library Personnel News* 8 (May-June 1994): 2-3.

Organizational studies of workplace violence have shown that what once was uncommon is becoming a reality. According to the National Safe Workplace Institute, the characteristics of a violence-prone workplace are: stressed workers, a high number of injury claims, understaffing or excessive demands for overtime, and frequent grievances filed by employees. Some suggestions for preventing workplace violence are: establish grievance procedures, establish a crisis plan, implement effective security procedures, train supervisors and staff on conflict resolution, and foster a supportive, harmonious work environment.

Albrecht, Steve. *Fear and Violence on the Job: Prevention Solutions for the Dangerous Workplace.* Durham, NC: Carolina Academic Press, 1997. 223pp.

This is one of the newest books on the market dealing with workplace violence. Zero-tolerance, a concept popular when dealing with violent situations, is one of the themes Albrecht stresses. He gives several examples of zero-tolerance statements that organizations can use as a model for their personal statement. Albrecht admits, however, that zero-tolerance is a difficult concept to enforce because it means different things to different people and sometimes management becomes hyper-vigilant and over reactions occur.

Allcorn, Seth. *Anger in the Workplace.* Westport: Quorum Books, 1994. 173pp.

Exploring anger and aggression in the workplace, Allcorn defines violence and gives solutions to defusing anger. One interesting chapter is on the use of the feeling of belonging as an anger intervention strategy. Working under pressure often results in a loss of attachment; therefore, management has to learn to respond to attachment needs even under the worst conditions. Allcorn contributes several suggestions and insights about the understanding of workplace anger and aggression.

Bachman, Ronet. *Violence and Theft in the Workplace.* Washington, DC: United States Department of Justice, Office of Justice Programs, Bureau of Justice Statistics, 1994. 2pp.

This short report contains a wealth of information. Using statistics from the National Crime Victimization Survey for the years 1987-1992, it was found that, on the average, crime in the workplace costs employers 1.7 million lost days of work each year and a dollar amount of 55 million in lost wages. Among the more interesting facts in the report is that men are more likely to be victims of a violent crime but women are more likely to experience theft. Six out of ten incidents occurred in private companies, and more than one-half of all workplace crimes were not reported to police.

Barron, Daniel D. "Violence, Schools, Society, and the School Library Media Specialist." *School Library Media Activities Monthly* 13 (March 1997): 47.

Barron discusses the role of education in solving the problem of violence in schools.

Bender, David L. *Is Violence a Serious Problem in America?* San Diego, CA: Greenhaven Press, 1996. 60pp.

This pamphlet presents opposing viewpoints on violence in the workplace. Six short chapters each focus on a different workplace violence issue, whether it is violent youth or whether violence is a serious crime or one blown out of proportion. Presented in point–counterpoint fashion, this pamphlet is very interesting and presents some refreshing beliefs.

Bensimon, Helen Frank. "Violence in the Workplace." *Training and Development* 27 (January 1994): 27-32.

Violence in the workplace is an increasing problem, and according to two experts in the field of workplace safety, Joseph Kinney and Dennis Johnson, in 1992 there were 111,000 incidents of workplace violence. These incidents cost employers $4.2 billion. Crime directed at employers or former employers constitutes the fastest growing type of workplace violence. The most common causes of violence towards employers are layoffs, mergers, and downsizing. Some work environments seem to encourage troubled employees. Characteristics of troubled work environments are chronic labor/management disputes, frequent grievances filed by employees, several stressed workers, understaffing, excessive overtime, and authoritarian management. Experts agree that potential workplace murderers hint that they are planning something. The profile of a typical workplace killer are a white male in his thirties/forties who has lost his job or perceives that he will soon lose his job, has been "let go" in an insensitive manner, is a loner, has a tendency to blame others for his problems, has a fascination with weapons, and repeatedly violates company policies and rules.

Bernstein, Andrea. "Workplace Violence A Growing Threat." *Newsday* (May 5, 1996): F12.

Homicide is the leading cause of death for women on the job and the second leading cause of workplace deaths. Regardless of these statements and supporting statistics from the United States Department of Justice, only 28% of United States companies have policies to deal with workplace violence. While some jobs are more conducive to workplace violence, domestic issues spill over into work and contribute to some violence. The Occupational Safety and Health Administration (OSHA) requires that an employer maintain a workplace that is free from recognized hazards. This puts pressure on organizations to ensure that their employees are safe and secure.

Berry, Wanda A. "Random Acts of Violence/Kindness." *LLA Bulletin* 59 (Winter 1996): 122-125.

Berry recounts a traumatic act of violence that robbed a DeSoto Parish library (Louisiana) of its veil of safety. During one spring weekend, a vandal entered the library and destroyed computers, VCRs and microfiche readers and broke windows. The vandal, a twenty-one-year-old man, was convicted of the crime, but the devastation of what happened will be with the community for years to come.

"Bomb Blast Jolts Library at Michigan's Oakland University." *American Libraries* 21 (March 1990): 180-181.

A bomb in the Oakland University Library was a rude awakening for Michigan residents to the prevalence of academic library violence. This article describes the incident.

Bowie, Vaughan. *Coping With Violence: A Guide for the Human Services.* Sydney, Australia: Karibuni Press, 1989. 172pp.

This book gives good, practical advice for the prevention of violence in the workplace. The primary focus is on human-service workers, an all-encompassing classification that includes teachers, police, doctors, nurses, social workers, and other professionals who have face-to-face contact with the public. There doesn't seem to be a single area left uncovered, and there are even several pages of photos illustrating various defenses or physical intervention techniques. The author cites pertinent Australian and British research that provides a basis for the book.

Braithwaite, Ray. *Violence, Understanding, Intervention, and Prevention.* Oxford, England: Radcliffe Professional Press, 1992. 136pp.

Working with the definition of violence as behavior which produces damaging or hurtful effects physically or emotionally on another person, the author takes the reader step-by-step through all phases of workplace violence. What are the physical and mental effects? How should acts of violent and aggressive behavior be handled? What are the responsibilities of line managers? The information that is given is practical and is accompanied by exercises designed to test one's skills at handling violent situations.

Burns, Philip D. *Multiple Victims, Multiple Causes: How to Recognize, Understand, and Stop the Disease of Violence within Our Homes, Schools, and Workplace.* Tulsa, OK: SyTech Research, 1995. 217pp.

If you can get past the very narrow margins and rather cramped layout, this book contains a wealth of information. Not only does Burns give facts and statistics, he also includes sample forms for reporting various threats and cases of injury or violence. An interesting addition is the "Pledge Against Violence," something that every office (or home) should have posted.

Capozzoli, Thomas and R. Steve McVey. *Managing Violence in the Workplace.* Delray Beach, FL: St. Lucia Press, 1996. 138pp.

Most of the workforce spends 35-65% of their waking time at work and during these hours, employees want to feel safe and free from threats and violence. The authors have taken a practical approach to the management of workplace violence. The first chapter is devoted to real-life case studies of workplace violence, and from there taxonomy, causes, profiles, and contributing factors of reducing workplace violence are explored. It is interesting to look at the factors contributing to workplace violence. Some of these are role conflict, lack of social support, changes that take place within the organization, work hours, and ergonomics.

Cronin, Michael P. "Workplace Violence: Defusing Dangerous Employees." *Inc.* 16 (October 1994): 124.

Cronin reports on advice given by Joan Acherstein, a lawyer with Jackson, Lewis, Schnitzler and Frupman in Boston. Acherstein outlines guidelines organizations should follow when dealing with workplace violence involving an employee. She also discusses the Americans with Disabilities Act (ADA) and what part it plays in protecting employees while still preserving a violent employee's rights.

Curry, Renee and Terry Allison. *States of Rage: Emotional Eruption, Violence, and Social Change.* New York: New York University Press, 1996. 268pp.

Rage. Exactly what is it? Lately, "road rage" has been a focus in reducing automobile violence. This book is a compilation of essays covering all types of rage, in all work settings. Chapter two, written by Dianne Layden, deals with violence, the emotionally enraged employee, and the workplace. Layden discusses the use of psychological tests for pre-employment screening.

D'Addario, Francis James. *The Manager's Violence Survival Guide.* Chapel Hill: Crime Prevention Associates, 1995. 74pp.

As a certified protection professional, D'Addario is well versed in workplace violence. This manual is a short, quick study of what to do to protect yourself and your organization from violence. Daunting statistics are interspersed throughout the chapters. One of the unique sections in this guide is the ABCs of personal violence avoidance. A few examples are: A is for awareness; Light the premises; Make eye contact; Words express intentions; and Zero-tolerance is not exclusively reserved for work.

Danford, Robert and Susan Cirillo. "Violence in the Library: Protecting Staff and Patrons." *Library Administration and Management* 11 (Spring 1997): 86-87.

The authors introduce a two-part special section on library violence. Recognizing that workplace violence is increasing and libraries are not immune to the same concerns as businesses, the authors express the sentiment that library management must become aware of the potential for violence in libraries.

David, Dennis A. *Threats Pending, Fuses Burning: Managing Workplace Violence.* Palo Alto: Davies-Black Publishing, 1997. 198pp.

Davis, a nationally recognized expert on violence prevention and intervention, has written a very thorough and practical book. It is divided into three parts: the problem and the perpetrators; prevention and intervention; and case studies and assessment. An overview of workplace violence is given in the first section. Prevention plans and sample policies are discussed in section two, and section three provides a chance to learn from others and try your hand at solving problems. Davis also gives a list of consultants to contact to assist with workplace violence issues. A questionnaire that allows organizations to assess their "violence quotient" is also included. To get his point across, Davis relates some hard-to-dispute statistics on workplace violence such as in 1994 there were 1,075 workplace homicides, and trends show that this number rises each year. Chapter eight is a must read because it gives the worst practices for dealing with workplace violence.

Davis, Donna G. "Security Problems in College and University Libraries: Student Violence." *College and Research Libraries* 32 (January 1971): 15-22.

Before reading this article, you need to look at the publication date and think about what was taking place on most university campuses at that time. It was a period of unrest, and libraries were among those targeted for violence. Davis' article is an excellent historical look not only at a volatile time at most universities but also at how innocent libraries, generally havens of peace and solitude, became focal points of violence.

DeBecker, Gavin. *The Gift of Fear: Survival Signals That Protect Us From Violence.* New York: Little, Brown, 1997.

DeBecker has developed a software package called MOSAIC that contains basic survival information on identifying risk behaviors of people who commit workplace violence, domestic violence, and stalking.

Dole, Wanda V. *The Literature of Library Violence, 1959-1989: An Annotated Bibliography.* Monticello, IL: Vance Bibliographies, 1990. 16pp.

This bibliography looks at thirty years of articles and monographs that focus on library security issues. The entries are alphabetical by author or title. Broad subject headings are used to divide the contents. Most of the citations cover problem patrons and disruptive behavior.

Duggar, David. "Violence in the Library: A Theme Issue." *LLA Bulletin* 59 (Winter 1996): 119-120.

Duggar presents an introduction to the winter issue of *LLA Bulletin*. Technological communication has broadened the public's awareness of violence.

Entrekin, Paulette D. "Crime and Violence in Mississippi Libraries: A Preventive Approach." *Mississippi Libraries* 59 (Summer 1995): 36-37.

Violent crime has not directly affected Mississippi libraries, but it is important to become aware of the rise in violent incidents occurring in the workplace. Awareness and preparedness are key to protecting staff and patrons from potential crimes.

Filipczak, Bob. "Armed and Dangerous at Work." *Training* 30 (July 1993): 42.

According to the United States Bureau of Labor statistics, homicides are the second most frequent cause of death in the workplace. Because many organizations are more aware of workplace violence, it is possible that a potentially dangerous employee can be identified and steps towards intervention taken before the employee explodes. What does one look for? The average dangerous employee is twenty-five to fifty years old and a loner, and tends to be a white male. Of course, there are exceptions to this profile. One of the most important things to remember is not to dismiss a disgruntled employee's threats, regardless of how idle they seem. The most obvious method of making sure violent employees are kept out of the workplace is by not hiring them. However, this isn't as easy as it sounds. Reference checks don't always prove to give the most truthful information, and the ADA protects people with a variety of disabilities, including mental illnesses, from discrimination.

Flannery, Raymond B. *Violence in the Workplace.* New York: Crossroad, 1995. 188pp.

Flannery, a licensed clinical psychologist and the author of two books on stress reduction, looks at workplace violence as being stress related. Set in two parts, the general nature of workplace violence and strategies for coping with workplace violence, this book examines the mind of the assailant, the disgruntled employee, stress management for employees, and how to debrief a victim and illustrates some relaxation exercises for both the perpetrator and the victim.

Grainger, Carol. *Violence: A Risk Management Handbook for Dealing with Violence at Work.* Brisbane, Australia: Mintinta Press, 1994. 125pp.

Grainger has written a comprehensive book on how to handle workplace violence. No longer can an organization afford to ignore the possibility of workplace violence. Designed for employees, managers, and employers, this account gives valuable advice for the moment when these individuals may be confronted with violence. Grainger purports that violence is something that "cannot be tolerated nor is it not inevitable, but it can be controlled by using a basic risk management approach." Grainger cites advice from a Queensland Division of Workplace Health and Safety publication, "Occupational Violence: Were You Threatened at Work Today?" One of the more interesting pieces is a risk assessment formula. Three variables are given: consequences, frequency, and severity. She closes with appendices giving ten commandments for reducing stress, along with additional stress management techniques.

Guerricagoitia, Ellen. "Bomb Threat Workshop Report." *The Unabashed Librarian* 95 (September 1995): 12.

In the case of a bomb threat, Guerricagoitia recommends these five tips: hang up the phone in order to clear your mind and get a grip on what is taking place; when the caller calls back, pay attention to the exact wording and note whether the caller is a male or female and any other details such as accent, etc.; when the caller hangs up, don't hang up — instead, try to have the call traced and use another line to call 911 to report the call; and if the building is evacuated, help the bomb squad by looking around your immediate area for anything that is out of place.

"Has Workplace Violence Become Part of Your Job?" *Library Personnel News* 8 (September-October 1994): 3-4.

Examples of types of violent and pre-violent incidents library workers have encountered while on the job include: threats, murder, hostage situations, stalking, shooting, gang violence, and assault with weapons. To assist in becoming more prepared to deal with violent incidents, librarians should solicit employee involvement, have a written plan for dealing with workplace violence, and regularly discuss incidents that have occurred and how the plan is working.

Heap, Jane. "Tackling Workplace Violence and Aggression in Bradford's Libraries." *Public Library Journal* 5 (May/June 1990): 81-82.

Heap's article describes the Bradford (England) Libraries' pro-active program to assist staff in dealing with difficult situations. Key areas were identified and used as the training focuses. These included coping with complaints, awareness of unacceptable behavior, how to report incidents, and personal safety.

Heskett, Sandra L. *Workplace Violence: Before, During, and After.* Boston: Butterworth-Heinemann, 1996. 202pp.

Heskett, who has a fifteen-year career as a security and safety coordinator, has written a thorough and detailed overview of workplace violence. She cites statistics, definitions, OSHA guidelines, and tips on what to do and relates real-life incidents. Stressed is the philosophy that reducing workplace violence starts at the top of the corporate ladder and should involve everyone. To help an organization get going on a workplace violence policy and procedure, Heskett provides a sample policy and procedure, examples of training programs and services, and information on background checks.

Johnson, Dennis L. "Workplace Violence, Why It Happens and What to Do About It." *EAP Digest* 10 (March/April 1994): 18-22.

Johnson takes the stance that workplace violence is a symptom of the pressures resulting from numerous social issues and corporate trends. How violent have we become? In the United States, you are seven times more likely to be murdered, one in ten eighth-graders has carried a weapon to school in the past thirty days, and an average of three people are murdered on the job every day. Yes, America is violent. The following factors have been found to be essential in protecting society from homicide: an economic system that provides full employment, a legal system that emphasizes prevention, and a cultural system that maintains a norm of good behavior.

Johnson, Dennis L., John B. Kiehlbauch, and Joseph A. Kinney. "Break the Cycle of Violence." *Security Management* 38 (February 1994): 24-28.

More organizations are beginning to establish a zero-tolerance policy for potentially violent behavior. This article suggests stopping violence at or before the threat stage. The authors remark that there is no "one size fits all" threat management plan. When drafting a threat management policy, it is important to include statements about activities that can lead to workplace violence. Issues such as sexual harassment, substance abuse, and possession of firearms should be covered. The first step in creating a theft management policy is a needs assessment that includes surveys of physical facilities, security systems, access to authorization programs, and existing security programs.

Johnson, Dennis L., John G. Kurutz, and John B. Kiehlbauch. "Scenario for Supervisors." *HR Magazine* 40 (February 1995): 63.

What would you do if you received an anonymous threatening note in your workplace mailbox? This article gives an overview of the steps an organization should take to address a potentially violent act. Using psychological profiles and sound management techniques, anyone is capable of pinpointing a potentially violent employee. This article is interesting and informative and gives good advice.

Kelleher, Michael D. *New Arenas for Violence: Homicide in the American Workplace.* Westport, CT: Praeger, 1996. 193pp.

More and more, occupational homicide is becoming an issue in all organizations. This book looks at the history, nature, and causes of murder in the workplace. Although the general nature of libraries is not conducive to violent crimes, the possibility still exists, and management should begin to address the issues before an incident occurs. Some suggestions for prevention of occupational homicide include performing background checks on potential new hires, structuring the termination process so it is less threatening, training employees in the job and making sure they are aware of safety and crises policies and procedures, holding safety and violence prevention meetings and workshops, and making sure employee assistance programs are available and known to employees.

— — —. *Profiling the Lethal Employee: Case Studies of Violence in the Workplace.* Westport, CT: Praeger, 1997. 155pp.

How does one know if an employee is potentially lethal? Kelleher provides information to help with understanding workplace violence and the people who commit the crimes. In 1993, the National Institute for Occupational Safety and Health (NIOSH) published the results of a long-term study on American worker fatalities. It was determined that homicide is a significant contributor to the death rate of American workers. During the 1980s, 63,589 workers died from job-related injuries with 14% homicides. More disconcerting is that homicide was the leading cause of death for women in the workplace. Who is the typical workplace murderer? Typically, the average perpetrator is under the age of thirty, male, and either a current or former employee, and used a firearm to commit the crime. Kelleher also gives case studies and suggests method of intervention and prevention.

Keller, Daniel P. "Special Problems in the Library Setting." *Library Administration and Management* 11 (Summer 1997): 161-165.

Violent actions in libraries are becoming more of a problem. Keller's article discusses the types of violence that pervade libraries, what the warning signs are, preventive measures, and other action the library can take to keep its collection and people secure.

Kinney, Joseph A. and Dennis L. Johnson. *Breaking Point.* Chicago: National Safe Workplace Institute, 1993. 115pp.

The Centers for Disease Control and Prevention (CDC) declared workplace homicide a serious public problem in 1992, and during 1992 there were 111,000 incidents of workplace violence in the United States. The first landmark case of workplace violence occurred in Edmond, Oklahoma on August 20, 1986 when a disgruntled postal worker killed thirteen of his co-workers. Kinney and Johnson discuss a three-system society: an economic system where there are high rates of unemployment, a legal system that has an inefficient criminal justice system and liberal gun laws, and a cultural system that glamorizes violence in popular culture. The authors have conducted a considerable amount of research to make this a comprehensive overview of the increasing problem of workplace violence. They also include a national sample of violent workplace incidents during a ten-year period, 1984-1993.

——— . *Violence at Work, How to Make Your Company Safer for Employees and Customers.* Englewood Cliffs, NJ: Prentice-Hall, 1995. 254pp.

Workplace violence involves a range of acts including homicide and intimidation. It is difficult to be productive and focus on our work if we feel threatened. Attacks, threats, and harassment are the three main types of workplace violence. In 1994 it was determined that there are approximately one million work crimes: 100,000 of these involved guns. These crimes are costly to corporations, law enforcement, and society. In general it is thought that workplace murders, rapes, and other serious forms of violence have a cost of $300,000 per occurrence. What can be done to protect employees from this violence? First, assess the weak spots; next, write an effective policy against this type of violence; communicate the policy to employees; establish teams to address threats; and know how to deal with dangerous employees. Kinney also looks at security measures such as cameras and buzzers.

——— . "When Domestic Violence Strikes the Workplace." *HR Magazine* 40 (August 1, 1995): 74.

Too often, domestic violence oversteps its boundaries and runs over into the office. A survey of security directors at 248 companies in twenty-seven states found that domestic violence is an increasing problem in many organizations. In fact, 94% ranked domestic violence "high" on a scale of security problems and 93%

reported that domestic violence was increasing. To help curtail the increase, organizations need to encourage their employees to report any threats they have received. Security offices also need to make sure they ask the right questions in order to assess the situation accurately. Local law enforcement personnel need to be informed of potential threats. Employees have the right to be safe and secure in their workplaces.

Labig, Charles E. *Preventing Violence in the Workplace.* New York: American Management Association, 1995. 196pp.

Preventing workplace violence is a complex challenge, and in this book the author looks at the rising incidents of violence occurring in the workplace and offers his idea of how to prevent more incidents. After giving the reader a solid background in workplace violence, Labig authoritatively states that organizations need to develop policies against violence and develop plans of action to avert violence. He purports that an essential ingredient in preventing workplace violence is identifying and responding to high-risk situations before they become violent. A risk assessment must be conducted, and from there an action plan should be written.

MacLeod, Marcia. "Violence in British Public Libraries." *The Unabashed Librarian* 56 (1985): 29-30.

This article is a short report on the rising violence to hit British libraries in the 1980s. Many libraries were forced to hire security guards to patrol the building, and others found they had to bolt their doors, only unlocking them when a legitimate patron requested entry. MacLeod gives several shocking examples of the violence that plagued British libraries.

Mantell, Michael and Steve Albrecht. *Ticking Bombs: Defusing Violence in the Workplace.* Burr Ridge, IL: Irwin Professional Publishing, 1994. 273pp.

Unfortunately, violence is becoming a common occurrence. A recent study by the American Psychological Association found that among first and second graders, 45% had witnessed muggings, 31% had witnesses shootings, and 39% had seen dead bodies. Mantell gives common sense and practical advice. His approach is based on a seven-step model that encompasses all of the visible and invisible factors surrounding workplace violence. These seven traits include pre-employment screening, an informed, aware management, management who understands the

"Golden Rule" of employee treatment, the value of educational programs for job and personal problems, proper security measures, and aftermath training. What is the "Golden Rule" of employee management? Treat your staff as you would like to be treated. This book also comes as a two-part training video.

McClure, Lynne Falkin. *Risky Business.* New York: Haworth Press, 1996. 208pp.

McClure's book raises awareness of workplace violence and offers tips on identifying high-risk employees. Eight types of potentially violent employees are characterized: actors, fragmentors, me-firsts, wooden sticks, mixed messengers, escape artists, shockers, and strangers. Along with these labels, McClure also gives the characteristic behaviors of these employees and explains each label.

Minor, Marianne. *Preventing Workplace Violence: Positive Management Strategies.* Menlo Park, CA: Crisp Publications, 1995. 85pp.

Instead of taking an in-depth look at workplace violence, this book is a short self-study. The author defines workplace violence and then takes the reader through facts about workplace violence, how to identify potentially violent employees (defensive, a marginal performer, holds a grudge, is frequently angry, sees the work environment as family), prevention strategies, and what to do if violence happens. Managers have a very important role in keeping the work environment safe. Limits on appropriate behavior need to be set, standards and policies should be enforced. Minor also discusses ten case studies that allow the reader to practice newly learned techniques.

Morrissey, James A. "Workplace Violence Rising." *Textile World* 146 (February 1996): 30-33.

Workplace violence has tripled during the past ten years, and each year more than one thousand people are murdered while at work. Additionally, two million are attacked, six million are threatened, and sixteen million are harassed. Stress and the tendency for people to get and use handguns and knives to settle differences are attributed to the increase in workplace violence. There are six steps an organization can take to anticipate and prevent workplace violence: 1) use good pre-employment screening; 2) adopt a well-thought out security program; 3) conduct training programs for first line and middle management; 4) be careful when handling terminations; 5) provide services such as counseling and employee assistance programs; and 6) consider allowing employees a stronger voice and let them share more power over their destinies. Some early warning signs of potentially violent behavior are deceit or veiled verbal threats, physical intimidation, paranoid behavior, moral righteousness, inability to take criticism of job performance, history of aggressive behavior, and expression of extreme desperation over recent family, financial, or personal problems.

Nelson, James. "Safety in the Public Library." *The Unabashed Librarian* 88 (1993): 9-13.

Libraries are subject to floods, tornadoes, earthquakes, and violence. Nelson discusses some of the steps a library should take to protect its patrons from injury.

O'Neill, James W. "From the Editor's Desk: Staff and Patron Safety — Eight Most Common Problems." *Library Security Newsletter* 1 (September/October 1975): 3-5.

According to the Enoch Pratt Free Library in Baltimore, Maryland, some of the most common disruptions in the library are unsafe parking lots, threat of personal injury, muggings, exhibitionists, malicious youth, and loitering.

Owsley, Beatrice Rodriguez. "Campus Violence: The Effects on the Campus Library." *LLA Bulletin* 59 (Winter 1996): 147-152.

Campus violence seemed to become more prevalent during the early 1940s. The 1960s proved to be another important period. Owsley reports that a segment of the university that is especially vulnerable to crime is the library. Academic libraries are generally isolated from clusters of other campus buildings and remain open into the late night. In addition to background information, Owsley also offers tips on controlling violence in the library setting.

Pantry, Sheila. *Dealing with Aggression and Violence in Your Workplace.* London: Library Association Publishing, 1996. 82pp.

Although this book has a definite British slant, its information knows no boundaries. Pantry starts out with short vignettes then poses the question, "Would you have known what to do in each incident?" Some of the issues covered are work-related aggression and violence, who is at risk, management responsibility, what to do if aggression is a threat, and writing an anti-harassment policy.

Pantry also gives a sample of an incident report that can serve as a template for libraries, as well as other organizations, to use.

Pease, Barbara. "Workplace Violence in Libraries." *Library Management* 16 (1995): 30-39.
    Pease states that most of the violence occurring in libraries has been caused by patrons, not staff. A library's long-standing role in public service accounts for the need for added security and discipline.

Preventing Workplace Violence: Guidelines for Preventing Violence in the Workplace, A Comprehensive Guide for School, Small Businesses, and Communities. St. Paul, MN: Minnesota Department of Children, Families and Learning, Office of Community Services, 1996. n.p.
    This loose-leaf publication gives a thorough look at procedures that address issues of workplace violence for school personnel. Even though the main focus is on the state of Minnesota and state-specific OSHA rules, this publication could serve as excellent background information and a template for other states. Included are guidelines for making school campuses safe, assessment tools, and tips on averting workplace violence. Also given are sample report forms that can be adapted to any agency.

Protection of Workers from Violence in the Workplace. Victoria, British Columbia: Public Service Employee Relations Commission, 1997. 44pp.
    This guide gives tips to use when developing a workplace violence protection program. Workplace violence knows no boundaries, and even though most published literature is about United States violence, our neighbor to the north has experienced the same increasing incidents. Included are risk assessment tools and a section on how to write a policy and procedure that communicate an anti-violence atmosphere. The appendices are especially helpful because they contain the Canadian Workers' Compensation Board regulations on protecting workers from violence.

Puderbaugh, Tom K. *Violence in the Workplace: Managing People in the Age of Rage!* Palm Harbor, FL: Development Dynamics, 1996. 93pp.
    Written by a management training consultant who specializes in workplace violence, this book takes a quick look at legal issues, pre-employment screening, employee assistance programs, surviving an encounter with an agitated person, creating a threat

management team, and developing policies and procedures. It isn't as well organized and easy to read as it should be, but considering it is designed to be a personal handbook, its informal layout is acceptable. For a very general, non-specific overview of workplace violence issues, this publication would fill the need. There are dozens of other handbooks that provide the same information in more detail.

RBC Limited. *A Handbook for the Prevention of Violence in the Workplace.* RBC Limited, 1996. n.p.

Although the title doesn't allude to it, this specially bound notebook focuses on workplace violence in the home health-care industry. Nonetheless, the information it contains is applicable to anyone. Some interesting inclusions are a list of winter storm supplies that should be carried in your car and NIOSH and OSHA guidelines for preventing workplace violence. This publication would be useful to consult if putting together your own handbook on workplace violence prevention.

RiCharde-Kreiner, Hadley. "A Georgia National Trend: Ways Sought to Protect Workers as On-the-Job Violence Increases." *The Atlanta Journal and Constitution* (July 5, 1997): E03.

Violence in the workplace is the second leading cause of death at work in Georgia and the United States. The CDC calls workplace violence "epidemic." Too often what may appear to be a very attentive boyfriend is actually a controlling person whose aggression proves to be fatal. It's important to remember that every business has the possibility of something happening that is violent.

Saker, Anne. "Another Front on Crime: Preventing Workplace Violence." *Gannett News Service* (February 2, 1994).

Found on the Internet, this news brief is a short, succinct story on OSHA's study on workplace violence. The change in thought is due to the rise in workplace homicide. The federal government is taking two approaches to workplace violence. One is the hiring of lawyer Susan Fox to study what the government can do to curtail this type of violence, and the other has to do with legislation that would strengthen a 1979 law on workplace violence.

Scharz, Eitan D. and Janice M. Kowalski. "Malignant Memories: Effect of a Shooting in the Workplace on School Personnel's Attitudes." *Journal of Interpersonal Violence* 8 (December 1993): 468-485.

This article reports the results of a study of twenty-four school personnel (twenty-two to sixty-six years of age), interviewed six to eighteen months following a shooting at the school. Interestingly, the subjects reported that they feel more positive since the shooting about their families, their community, and their workplace.

Segal, Jonathan A. "When Charles Manson Comes to the Workplace." *HR Magazine* 39 (June 1994): 33-38.

Segal covers employer liability, pre-employment practices, and post-employment security measures. In general, violent behaviors are divided into three categories: violence directed to a third party by an employee, violence directed to another employee, and a combination of these two. When considering steps to take before hiring someone, management needs to be aware of its responsibility to maintain a safe workplace and to avoid negligent hiring claims. First, management may want to conduct criminal record checks and drug testing and structure interview questions that would elicit responses that provide insight into a propensity for violence. Once someone is hired, the organization can have a safety policy prohibiting workplace violence and rules that minimize the likelihood of workplace violence occurring, provide sufficient training to supervisors, establish a crisis management team, and make use of psychiatric assessments when appropriate.

"SHRM Reveals Extent of Workplace Violence." *EAP Digest* (March/April 1994): 25.

Out of 1,000 surveys sent to Society of Human Resource Management (SHRM) members, one-third declared that their workplace had experienced a violent incident in the past five years (1989-1994). In fact, 44% responded that an act of violence took place in their workplace during 1993. Guns were involved in 17%, and 75% involved a fistfight or other physical altercation. Personality conflicts, family/marital problems, and alcohol or other drug abuse accounted for the majority of the violent occurrences. Summer saw the most reports of violence, with November-January as having the least.

Sprouse, Martin. *Sabotaging the American Workplace.* San Francisco: Pressure Drop Press, 1992. 175pp.

The author relates his disturbing discussions with employees who committed theft, vandalism, sabotage, and other heinous crimes. After reading some of the employees' comments, you will think twice about making your co-worker mad at you.

Stennett-Brewer, Linda. *Violence in the Workplace: Risk Reduction and Management.* Bloomington, IL: Lighthouse Institute, 1994. 58pp.

Brewer-Stennett, an employee assistance program consultant for Caterpillar, Inc. has firsthand experience in management techniques for reducing workplace violence. Over the years, Caterpillar has undergone several re-organizations and has had to lay off employees. This book is concerned with violence committed by current or past employees and not those acts of violence committed by non-employees. Not only has the American Bar Association made public statements about the legal, moral, and ethical issues that have arisen from workplace violence, but OSHA has also been very vocal and recently started to respond to reports of violence. The author presents an overview of incidents and covers employer liability, risk assessment, establishing a crisis risk management program, and what tactics can be used if a violent act does occur. The advice is practical and can be easily followed by any organization.

Strategies for Preventing Workplace Violence and Harassment. Berkeley, CA: California Continuing Education of the Bar, 1995. 130pp.

This monograph is the handbook used in a 1995 program on workplace violence and harassment that the California Continuing Education of the Bar sponsored. Although the text has a definite legal slant, the layman would also benefit from reading it. In addition to court cases involving workers compensations, intentional misconduct, and negligent hiring and retention, also presented are the OSHA guidelines for workplace security. Nearly every area of workplace security is explained, including a lengthy section on sexual harassment.

Taylor, Ronald W. "The Rockem-Sockem Workplace." Http://venable.com/wlu/rockem.htm (September 24, 1997).

A 1993 survey conducted by Northwestern National Life Insurance Company showed that each year 2.2 million workers are physically attacked, 6.3 million are threatened, and 16.1 million are harassed. These figures are astounding and they are on the rise.

Thomas, Janice L. "Occupational Violent Crime: Research on an Emerging Issue." *Journal of Safety Research* 23 (Summer 1992): 55-62.

Even though this article focuses on convenience store violence, it has pertinence to today's library because many libraries house coffee shops, canteens, and photocopy centers that deal in cash transactions, just like convenience stores. This study found that at-risk work sites were those that required an exchange of money in a low security environment.

Twilling, Greg. *What Will Be the Role of Law Enforcement in Workplace Violence by the Year 2004?* Sacramento, CA: State of California, Department of Justice, 1995. 130pp.

This book is a technical report used as part of the teaching materials for a peace officer standards and training class. Twilling examines violence as it appears in the American workforce. The primary factors studied are what types of training programs will reduce workplace violence, what technological advancements will ensure a safe workplace environment, and what policies will aid law enforcement in the intervention of the violence. This book gives a good police officer's view and stresses the importance of the partnership between a police force and the community.

"Violence in Libraries." *Library Association Record* 89 (April 1987): 201.

The British Library Association established a working group to study the problem of violence, vandalism, and abusive behavior in libraries. The group's intent is to draft guidelines aimed at staff and management in libraries. Included will be training sessions and notes on how to handle difficult situations.

"Violence in the Workplace." *Library Association Record* 93 (July 1991): 426.

This short article discusses the report on workplace violence that the Suzy Lamplugh Trust sponsored. The report reaffirms that aggression is not isolated to just one or two incidents; instead, it is a serious problem for all staff who have contact with the public.

Violence in the Workplace. Salem, OR: Department of Consumer and Business Services, 1996. 11pp.

This short pamphlet packs a lot of important information into its eleven pages. In addition to giving background information on workplace violence, it also gives steps an employer should take to prevent violence from impacting employees. Conduct an initial assessment of the business including hiring and termination procedures.

"Violence on the Job." *The Unabashed Librarian* 102 (1997): 24.
Excerpted from an article in the March 16, 1996, *New York Times*, this summary provides guidelines for employers to follow to reduce workplace violence. Suggestions include install metal detectors, use bright and effective lighting, use curved mirrors in hallways, and allow for two exits.

Violence Prevention Resource Manual. Portland, OR: Oregon Health Division: Multnomah County Health Department, 1996. Various pages.
This is a very complete, well-indexed, loose-leaf resource manual. Recognizing that violence is a major public health concern, the state of Oregon compiled this as a guide to assist with the development and implementation of violence prevention activities and programs. The manual is divided into color-coded sections, covering topics such as child abuse, domestic violence, workplace violence, and youth violence. Also included is a list of resources and a sample policy organizations can use when writing an organizational statement against workplace violence.

Wheat, Stella I. and Joy Greiner. "Violence in Mississippi's Public Libraries: 1995 Survey Results." *Mississippi Libraries* 59 (Summer 1995): 32-35.
Wheat and Greiner describe a survey about violence in public libraries sent to forty-seven public library directors in Mississippi. The survey determined the number of instances of violence, the type of violence, and what effect the violent act had on programs and staff. This is a very thorough look at the issues of violence that affect Mississippi libraries.

Wheeler, Eugene D. and S. Anthony Baron. *Violence in Our Schools, Hospitals and Public Places.* Ventura, CA: Pathfinder, 1994. n.p.
This book gives some startling evidence about violence in our schools and other public businesses.

Weisberg, Daniel. "Preparing for the Unthinkable." *Management Review* 83 (March 1994): 58-61.

"Plan ahead" is the motto Weisberg espouses. Because statistics show that violence happens in the workplace at an alarming rate, employers need to ensure that their employees are safe and violence-free. Who is the violent employee? The profile is a white male, age thirty- five to fifty, who has outside pressures. What can be done? Some organizations use psychological tests, but their effectiveness at screening individuals with the capacity to commit violent acts has never been proven. Additionally, the ADA rendered these tests illegal. Polygraph tests are also not as good an idea, but the actual interview can be structured to allow the employer to find out everything there is to know about the prospective employee. It is legal to ask about felony and misdemeanor convictions, and background checks have proven to be valuable. Regardless of the measures taken before hiring an employee, violent acts can still occur. To alleviate or lessen these occurrences, the organization should prohibit threats and intimidation, investigate all threats, employ managers who are trained in handling violent employees, develop an emergency plan, and make use of security systems.

Wellinger, Patricia. "Workplace Violence: Is Your Library at Risk?" *Colorado Libraries* 23 (Spring 1997): 16-18.
Criminal violence in libraries is not new, and it seems that each year more incidents are reported. Wellinger gives an overview of workplace violence and how libraries can better protect themselves. Employee warning signs are attendance problems, decreased productivity, unusual and changed behavior, inconsistent work patterns, and continual excuses or blaming others. Wellinger also gives some tips that may reduce the escalation of conflicts. These are: be empathetic, respect personal space, be aware of body position, permit verbal venting when possible, avoid overreacting, ignore challenge questions, set and enforce reasonable limits, and keep nonverbal cues non-threatening.

Willits, Robert L. "When Violence Threatens the Workplace." *Library Administration & Management* 11 (Spring 1997): 166-171.
Willits contends that violence is a reality one must be prepared for. A library has a fundamental obligation to both its patrons and staff to let them know they don't have to fear for their personal safety. Willits suggests a three-tiered approach to preventing and managing violence: outlining preventive measures, drafting a threat management plan, and establishing a crisis/post-trauma management team.

Workplace Violence. St. Paul, MN: Minnesota Continuing Legal Education, 1996. n.p.

This publication is a handbook used for a Minnesota Continuing Legal Education course. Divided into sections, it covers the gamut of workplace violence issues. It is well documented and cites appropriate code sections. Also included are interesting "Current Intelligence Bulletins" from the United States Department of Health and Human Services that cover violence in the workplace. Although the original audience was made up of attorneys and paralegals, the handbook would still be a valuable resource for management.

Workplace Violence: A BNA Plus Information Package. Washington, DC: BNA Plus, 1996. n.p.

This Bureau of National Affairs (BNA) loose-leaf service is a four-section manual that contains BNA guidelines, OSHA administrative documents, information on employee rights, and a bibliography. It is concise and thorough and includes some examples of staff assessment studies that can be used to gather information on how safe employees feel, how they feel towards administration, and how they feel towards one another.

Workplace Violence and Harassment. Arlington, VA: Security Management, 1994. 50pp.

This publication is a compilation of articles previously published in *Security Management.* Fifteen articles on violence, sexual harassment, and prevention techniques are reprinted. One is on the effects solvents have on people's bodies also investigates the effects these chemicals have on behavior. Another focuses on the risks imposed when an organization downsizes. Downsizing is an emotionally charged event and potential trouble can be headed off with a preventative action plan.

Problem Patrons

Askin, Frank. "Why All Sides Smelled Victory in Morristown Library Case." *New Jersey Libraries* 25 (Fall 1992): 9-12.

When Richard Kreimer sued the Joint Free Public Library of Morristown, New Jersey, for denied access, the library world came under scrutiny. Public libraries are generally thought to provide services to all people, regardless if they are homeless. When Kreimer was denied access due to his poor personal hygiene, the library's code of conduct was challenged. This article is a thorough look at all sides of this controversial lawsuit.

Baker, Zachary M. "Problem Patrons and Problem Librarians." *Judaica Librarianship* 6 (Spring 1991-Winter 1992): 168-171.

Humility and intellectual honesty are needed in times of dealing with problem patrons. Baker gives a personal, real-life example of a reference interview that went awry and offers suggestions on how he could have made it more positive.

Ballard-Thrower, Rhea. "Kreimer v. Morristown." *The Georgian Librarian* 29 (Spring 1992): 9-11.

This article is an analysis of various library policies and constitutional issues these policies are associated with. There are many aspects of the Kreimer lawsuit that are unfortunate, but one of the positive outcomes is that it has forced libraries to review their policies.

Barsumyan, Silva E. and P. Charles Livermore. "The Problem Patron." *New Jersey Libraries* 21 (Spring 1988): 1-4.

Librarians need to get tough with patrons who are bothersome and causing a disturbance. This article offers guidelines for handling problem patrons. New Jersey statutes are cited.

Bashear, J. Kirk, James J. Maloney, and Judellen Thornton-Jaringe. "Problem Patrons: The Other Kind of Library Security." *Illinois Libraries* 63 (April 1981): 343-351.

Two hundred twenty-eight Illinois libraries were surveyed regarding incidents of problem patrons. Seventy-two percent of the respondents reported one or more disruptive events — some that were harmless, but others that were violent. Intervention by library staff or security guards was the most common method of control.

Bryan, Gordon. "Tom: The Liberated Skeleton." *Emergency Librarian* 10 (March/April 1983): 12-15.

Covering the years 1969-1981, this annotated bibliography surveys the literature dealing with problem patrons. Policy statements and some unpublished works are cited.

"Bush Telegraph on Library Behaviour." *The Daily Telegraph* (November 25, 1997).

This short column cites incidents of unacceptable library behavior occurring in various British libraries. One case involved a female patron who dressed in a mini skirt and draped herself over several desks while remarking, "We must try to make this place sexy. . ."

Caparelli, Felicia. "Public Library or Psychiatric Ward? It's Time for Administrators to Deal Firmly with Problem Patrons." *American Libraries* 15 (April 1984): 212.

Problem patrons are no longer an issue that cannot be dealt with. Caparelli stresses the importance of library administration in dealing with problem patrons before the concern gets out of hand.

Chadbourne, Robert. "Disorderly Conduct: Crime and Disruptive Behavior in the Library." *Wilson Library Bulletin* 68 (March 1994): 23-26.

As odd as it may seem, libraries are at an increasing risk of being vulnerable to violence. Not only is security usually low, but most libraries are open nights and weekends and are seen as a gathering place or hangout. In order to position themselves so they are less vulnerable, librarians need to adjust their attitude and not allow the public to practice behaviors that are disruptive and potentially harmful. Chadbourne recommends that certain risks should be erased.

— — — . "The Problem Patron: How Much Problem, How Much Patron?" *Wilson Library Bulletin* 64 (June 1990): 59-60.

Chadbourne is well known in the library security field. He brings his expertise in perspective as he writes about the Worcester (Massachusetts)public library's policy on dealing with difficult patrons. The policy is well written, straightforward, and clear-cut.

Conable, Gordon M. "Access and Indigency: Lessons From Morristown." *Public Libraries* 31 (January/February 1992): 29-32.

This article takes a more legalistic approach to summarizing the Kreimer v. Morristown Public Library lawsuit than many others that have been published.

DeRosa, Frank J. "The Disruptive Patron." *Library & Archival Security* 3 (1980): 29-37.

If you want some practical advice and tips on dealing with irate and irrational patrons, read this article. The author, a security officer with twenty-one-years experience, writes in a clear and straight forward manner. DeRosa remarks that those individuals who disturb others in a public building are in violation of state statutes.

Dowd, Frances Smardo. *Latchkey Children in the Library & Community: Issues, Strategies, and Programs.* Phoenix, AZ: Oryx Press, 1991. 214pp.

Libraries seem to be safe havens for children; however, special care should be taken to ensure the children's safety. Dowd assists educators, librarians, parents, and other professionals in understanding latchkey children and their needs. Unsupervised children's safety is at risk, whether at home or in a library. Chapter seven focuses on innovative and successful strategies libraries are using to address the needs of latchkey children.

Driscoll, Alice. "Dilemma for Today's Public Librarian: The Problem Patron." *Southeastern Librarian* 15 (Spring 1980): 15-21.

Using the definition that a problem patron is one with aberrant sexual or emotional behavior, Driscoll reports how librarians deal with problem patrons and what areas of the library tend to be focal points for problems. The children's section is a focal point because they tend to be noisy. Restrooms are another location of various undesirable activities. Driscoll states that it is up to each librarian to take positive action when an incident occurs that threatens either a staff member or a patron. She continues to recommend that library directors should take action to discover what potential problems exist and then take the appropriate action to remedy those problems. Good rapport with the police department is essential, as is a statement of purpose and a policy on problem patrons. Driscoll's article offers timeless advice that should be considered by all library directors and security managers.

Easton, Carol. "Sex and Violence in the Library: Scream a Little Louder, Please." *American Libraries* 8 (October 1977): 484-488.

This article details the types of problems the Los Angeles Public Library faces. Easton suggests that librarians be "trained to be helping, caring, tolerant public servants."

Gold, Gerald. "Discipline in Libraries." *Encyclopedia of Library and Information Science* 7 (1972): 216.

Most instances of dealing with problem patrons amount to noise or children fighting; however, as Gold asserts, when trouble really brews, the police tend to be slow to respond.

Goldberg, Beverly. "Morristown Wins Appeal, but Kreimer Seeks Rehearing." *American Libraries* 23 (May 1992): 351-352.
Goldberg presents a short synopsis about the appeal ruling in the Kreimer v. Morristown Public Library case.

Griffith, Jack W. "Of Vagrants and Vandals and Library Things." *Wilson Library Bulletin* 52 (June 1978): 169.
Too often library staff are called upon to calm a disruptive patron, diffuse a volatile situation, or worse yet, try to talk a threatening patron out of the anger he or she is showing. Griffith notes that librarians are not trained social workers, nor are they psychiatrists, but many times they have to act like one.

Groark, James J. "Assertion: A Technique for Handling Troublesome Library Patrons." *Catholic Library World* 51 (November 1979): 172-173.
Behavior in a library isn't always one of a quiet nature. Too often, one's behavior is raucous, intimidating, or threatening. Groark's article gives some helpful tips on how to stand up to a library patron who is exhibiting unwanted behavior. Even though this article is twenty years old, the information is still timely and pertinent to today's library and the potential violence that can occur.

Grotophorst, Clyde W. "The Problem Patron: Toward a Comprehensive Response." *Public Library Quarterly* 1 (Winter 1979): 345-353.
Public libraries serve just that — the public. Among these patrons are people of all ages, and while the vast majority pose no problems at all, some are very real threats. Grotophorst reports that 50% of all police problems involve youth under the age of sixteen.

Hammeke, Nancy Byouk. "Kreimer vs Morristown: We Lived Through It and Won!" *New Jersey Libraries* 25 (Fall 1992): 12-15.
Hammeke's article is an excellent summary of one of the more controversial lawsuits to impact libraries. It is a firsthand account of the case, as seen through a library director's eyes.

Hankes, G.C. "Handling Problem Patrons: Help From an Osh-kosh In-Service Training Project." *Wilson Library Bulletin* 74 (September 1978): 210-212.

Staff training is extremely important when it comes to handling problem patrons. A well-informed staff can defuse some incidents before they become explosive. Hankes gives pointers from a staff training program on handling potential and real problem situations.

Hecker, Thomas E. "Patrons with Disability or Problem Patrons: Which Model Should Librarians Apply to People with Mental Illness?" *The Reference Librarian* 53 (1996): 5-12.

Too often, patrons with mental disabilities are treated as problem patrons, when instead they should be treated as patrons with disabilities. Hecker presents a practical approach to serving the mentally ill patron that couples understanding with accommodation.

Kaplan, Ruth L. *Disruptive Conduct in Libraries: Legal and Practical Responses to Sexual Harassment and Problem Patrons.* Boston: Proprietors of the Social Law Library, 1993. 436pp.

This is a large collection of previously published articles and policies on problem patrons and sexual harassment. Supporting chapters reiterate some state statutes on crime and security. This publication is a very thorough sourcebook for anyone wanting to write a security policy.

Landrum, Janet. "Working With the Violent Patron." *LLA Bulletin* 59 (Winter 1996): 135-140.

The violent patron that Landrum refers to is the violent institutionalized patient. Landrum describes the Southeast Louisiana Hospital and her experiences as librarian for the facility. The article is an excellent one to read to gather more insight into a type of library user that many public and academic libraries don't service.

"Local Press Defends Ann Arbor PL Behavior Rules Banning Problem Patrons." *American Libraries* 16 (January 1985): 7.

This short news clip cites the various support the Ann Arbor (Michigan) Public Library received for its proposed ban on sleepy and extremely smelly patrons. The new rules also prohibit fighting, drugs, weapons, gambling, alcoholic beverages, and harassment.

McNeil, Beth and Denise Johnson. *Patron Behavior in Libraries: A Handbook of Positive to Negative Solutions.* Chicago: American Library Association, 1996. 160pp.

The editors of this book envisioned that it would be used by library staff to help solve problems. Covered are descriptions of patrons that cause the most challenges, security issues in libraries, and possible solutions to alleviate negative behavior.

Martin, Susan K. "Order in the Library: Part II." *Library Issues* 7 (March 1987).

Poor acoustics, lack of space for socializing, and lack of respect for the libraryare causes for disruptive behavior. Martin takes an interesting viewof discipline when she mentions that librarians disciplining students or faculty doesn't bode well on campus.

Morrissett, Linda A. "Developing and Implementing a Behavior Policy for an Academic Library." *College and Undergraduate Libraries* 1 (1994): 71-91.

Morrissett discusses the importance of a policy on problem patrons in academic libraries. She covers conducting a needs assessment, the benefits of a behavior policy, writing corrective action statements, recording incidents, and considerations for special circumstances.

"Morristown Ruling Reversed." *Newsletter on Intellectual Freedom* 41 (May 1992): 73-74.

This is an interesting piece about the reversal of the controversial lawsuit Richard Kreimer brought against the Morristown Public Library.

Nelson, Dale. "Library of Congress Tackles Problem Patrons." *Wilson Library Bulletin* 54 (June 1980): 665.

The staff at the Library of Congress took a nineteen-week course on dealing with problem patrons. This article is a report on the course and the benefits it had on the library, the staff, and the service they provide.

Nelson, W.D. "Ban on Sleeping and Smelling." *Wilson Library Bulletin* 59 (March 1985): 468.

Nelson gives a quick summary of putting a stop to the plight some libraries face when transients use them as places to sleep.

———. "LC Tackles Problem Patrons." *Wilson Library Bulletin* 54 (June 1980): 655.

Problem patrons are not only an issue for academic and public libraries; the Library of Congress also has its share. Nelson discusses the issue and describes the steps the Library of Congress has taken to put a stop to the problem.

Owens, Sheryl. "Proactive Problem Patron Preparedness." *Library & Archival Security* 12 (1994): 11-23.

Owens uses real-life examples to illustrate problem patron situations. The author believes that library staff should be well versed in what to do and a pro-active plan must be in place. Deviant sexual behavior is also covered.

Reavis, Jennifer. "Patron Relations: A Transformational Approach." *Texas Libraries* 50 (Winter 89/90): 132-135.

The author takes a look at communicating with library patrons in a positive and helpful manner. Communication can be labeled as either constructive or destructive. Some constructive communication skills are to avoid jargon, show interest, ask questions to get more information, and look directly at the patron. Negative or destructive communication skills include failing to listen carefully, acting indifferent, or showing no interest. Interaction with irate patrons calls for using positive or constructive communication skills.

Revill, Don. "Library Security." *New Library World* 79 (April 1978): 75-77.

Problem patrons can exhibit different types of behavior. Some patrons cause disturbances, and others may mutilate library materials. Revill's article discusses the different types of problem patrons, and suggests that many are not anti-library, but are, instead, "pro themselves."

Rubin, Rhea Joyce. "Anger in the Library: Defusing Angry Patrons at the Reference Desk (and Elsewhere)." *Reference Librarian* 31 (1990): 39-51.

If you want practical information on how to deal with angry patrons, this article is for you. Rubin focuses on reference desk confrontations, but her advice can be used in all library settings. Be sure to look at the bibliography and reference list at the end of the article for sources to consult.

Sable, Martin. "Problem Patrons in Public and University Libraries." *Encyclopedia of Library and Information Science* 43 (1988): 169-179.

Problems with patrons have been a reality in libraries for years. Sable covers the types of problem patrons, gives a statistical analysis, and discusses the importance of having a policy pertaining to problem patrons and providing adequate training to staff.

Salter, Charles A. and Jeffrey L. Salter. *On the Frontlines: Coping with the Library's Problem Patrons.* Englewood, CO: Libraries Unlimited, 1988. 170pp.

As a service organization, libraries are visited by a wide variety of people. This monograph looks at nearly every kind of patron. The book is divided into two parts: part one is devoted to twenty-four case studies, all true events, and part two takes a look at how to cope with problem patrons. Also included are samples of problem patron documentation forms. Part one is very thorough and has discussion questions at the end of each case study.

Sampson, Karen. "Disturbed and Disturbing Patrons: Handling the Problem Patron." *Nebraska Library Association Quarterly* 8 (Spring 1982): 9-11.

The University of Nebraska developed a three-part seminar on establishing policies and increasing staff awareness of problem patrons. Sampson details this seminar and offers solutions to handling disturbing patrons.

Savage, Noel. "The Troublesome Patron: Approaches Eyed in New York." *Library Journal* 103 (December 1978): 2371-2374.

This article is filled with valuable information from security experts on how to keep library staff safe. All facets of the problem patron are looked at.

Shuman, Bruce. "Problem Patrons in Libraries— A Review Article." *Library & Archival Security* 9 (1989): 3-19.

Shuman takes an in-depth look at problem patrons in this article.

— — —. *River Bend Revisited: The Problem Patron in the Library.* New York: Oryx Press, 1984. 186pp.

Shuman has written a handbook that uses forty problem situations to illustrate the types of security problems that can arise in a public library setting. Using role-playing, the author explores solutions and encourages the reader to participate actively. This book is the continuation of the 1981 *River Bend Casebook*.

"Skunks, Drunks and Rights: A Discussion of Library Patron Policies." *The Sourdough* 29 (Spring 1992): 17.

This is a report of a panel discussion centered on the Kreimer v. Morristown Public Library lawsuit. The discussion brought up several issues that seem to fall into a gray area when it comes to constitutional rights.

Smith, Nathan and Irene Addonis. "Using Active Listening to Deal with Problem Patrons." *Public Libraries* 30 (July/August 1991): 236-239.

Good communication skills are important in any job. In this article, the authors give scenarios that explicitly show what happens when active listening skills are employed.

Sonnichsen, C.L. "A Real-Life Gothic Dracula in the Stacks." *Wilson Library Bulletin* 51 (January 1977): 419-423.

This article is included not solely because its title is catchy, but because it touches on a different type of annoyance — the bothersome patron. Although these patrons seldom cause problems of a security or criminal nature, they still cause problems because their excessive questions put an undue burden on the librarians' time. Lonely, chatty patrons can be threatening and this article takes a close look at "vampires," or those patrons whose questions make excessive demands on library staff.

Squibb, Molly, Rich Patton, and Linda Cumming. "Security Service with a Human Touch." *Colorado Libraries* 23 (Spring 1997): 6-8.

More and more libraries are finding themselves serving as daytime shelters for the homeless. Some of the homeless use the library's newspapers to find jobs, while others seem to cause a disturbance because they are dirty. This article looks at the fine line of rights of staff and patrons versus the constitutional right of all people to have access to information.

Taylor, Alan. "Flyleaf Dealing With Problem Patrons." *Scottish Libraries* 3 (May 1987): 17.

Taylor has written a tongue-in-cheek article comparing Ian Rankin's novel, *Knots and Crosses,* with problem patrons.

Timko, Lola C. "Teaching Communication with Problem Patrons in Emergency Situations." *Journal of Education for Librarianship* 18 (Winter 1978): 244-246.
Proper training of library staff can be the best weapon against disruptive patrons. Timko shares practical advice on how to deal with unexpected situations.

"Trouble at the Reference Desk." *Harper's Magazine* 295 (November 1997): 32.
Problem patrons in public libraries receive attention in this article. Different classes or types of problem patrons are detailed in chart form.

Turner, Anne M. *Problem Situations, Not Patrons.* Jefferson, NC: McFarland, 1993. 197pp.
Many library problem patron incidents are really problem situations. Latchkey children, street people, and sexual deviates create problem situations. Turner's book delves into dealing with problem situations and provides guidance on writing library rules and procedures on library exhibits and room reservations.

Uhler, Scott and Philippe Weiss. "Behave Yourself, This Is a Public Library!" *Illinois Libraries* 77 (Fall 1995): 189-191.
This article takes a look at the New Jersey public library lawsuit brought by Richard Kreimer, a homeless person. It gives an interesting viewpoint on the outcome of the case and presents guidelines for librarians to follow, as presented by Chicago attorneys.

Vocino, Michael Jr. "The Library and the Problem Patron." *Wilson Library Bulletin* 50 (January 1976): 372-373, 415.
Dealing with problem patrons sometimes forces a librarian to perform functions that he or she has not been trained to do. Vocino asserts that librarians must reassess what their jobs are and realize that they are not trained to be mental health counselors.

Wright, G.S. "America's First Library Kept Patrons Awake." *Wilson Library Bulletin* 32 (May 1958): 649.
Wright relates the story of the first example of regulating patron behavior.

Sexual Harassment

Fitzgerald, Louise F., S.L. Shullman, N. Bailey, M. Richards, J. Swecker, Y. Gold, M. Ormerod, and L. Weitzman. "The Incidence and Dimensions of Sexual Harassment in Academia and the Workplace." *Journal of Vocational Behavior* 32 (1988): 152-175.

This article uses research that was supported by a grant from the United States Department of Education. It is a thorough presentation of sexual harassment in academia, as documented by a study of 2,599 students.

——— . "Sexual Harassment: Violence against Women in the Workplace." *American Psychologist* 48 (October 1993): 1070-1076.

Using a survey that says one out of every two women will be harassed at some time during her academic or working career, this article takes an in-depth look at the prevalence and consequences of sexual harassment and outlines social policy implications. Sexual harassment has been present in working life since the 1700s, but not until the past few years has sexual harassment been brought into focus as a problem. Fitzgerald has thoroughly researched and clearly presented the facts that describe the prevalence of sexual harassment. She also tests legislative initiatives that would require employers to emphasize prevention of sexual harassment. Some suggestions the author gives include: require employers to develop a clear policy against harassment, and require organizations to notify employees of the policy, post it, and provide education and training; remove caps on available damages, and consider ways to encourage the award of substantial punitive damages that fit the seriousness of the offense; reform unemployment compensation statutes to ensure that women who quit their jobs due to harassment can receive unemployment compensation, and ensure that the legal system does not continue to re-victimize harassment victims.

Fried, N. Elizabeth. *Sex, Laws and Stereotypes: Authentic Workplace Anecdotes and Practical Tips for Dealing with the Americans with Disabilities Act, Sexual Harassment, Workplace Violence, and Beyond.* Shawnee Mission, KS: National Press Publication, 1995. 137pp.

This book is a catchall of workplace issues that affect both employers and employees. It gives a very thorough look at how to deal with these rules and regulations while still running a successful business. The author uses anecdotes to explain positions, and at the end of each she gives tips on what can be learned from the reported scenario. Some of the more important tips include knowing which Equal Employment Opportunity Commission (EEOC) laws affect your workplace, institute policies against workplace violence and sexual harassment, document all incidents, remember that confidentiality is important, and educate and train staff on these issues.

Gasaway, Laura N. "Sexual Harassment in the Library." *North Carolina Libraries* 49 (Spring 1991): 14-17.
   Title VII of the Civil Rights Act of 1964 offers protection against discrimination and governs all employers. Sexual harassment constitutes sexual discrimination and can occur between women and between men but more often is between men and women. The enforcing agency, the EEOC, has written guidelines that define sexual harassment. Several court cases provide support for the author's statements.

Goodson, Jane, Christine W. Lewis, and Renee D. Culverhouse. "Sexually Harassed and Stressed Out: The Employer's Potential Liability." *Journal of Managerial Issues* 6 (December 22, 1994): 428-444.
   Goodson reports that recent trends show that employees face large damage awards for stress-related consequences arising from sexual harassment. Pointing out that in 1991 sexual harassment claims increased 70% from the year prior, the authors note that even though court decisions display a wide range of views, there is a common ground that liability exists when management knew sexual harassment was occurring. Workers' compensation claims are also discussed with an increase in stress-related incidents being reported. Dozens of court cases support the authors' statements.

Goodyear, Mary Lou and William K. Black. "Combating Sexual Harassment: A Public Service Perspective." *American Libraries* 22 (February 1991): 134-136.
   Incidents of sexual harassment occur in libraries more often than anyone would like to admit. It is often difficult to determine whether some unwanted behavior is sexual harassment or an annoyance. Goodyear and Black expand on the issue of sexual harassment and describe Iowa State University Libraries' pro-active steps towards putting a stop to sexual harassment incidents. Included is Iowa State University's policy on harassment.

Gutch, B.A. and M.P. Koss. "Changed Women and Changed Organizations: Consequences of and Coping with Sexual Harassment." *Journal of Vocational Behavior* 42 (1993): 28-48.

The effects of sexual harassment on women who experience
sexual abuse and the morale, work behavior, and productivity of
organizations are studied in this article. Gutch and Koss report on
a composite of real experiences and illustrate a worst-case scenario. Sexual harassment has been a workplace issue for several
years, and a 1981 study has shown that one in ten left their jobs as
a result of sexual harassment. Some of the negative work-related
outcomes include lower self-esteem, decreased feelings of com-
petence, and less job satisfaction. The victim, however, isn't the
only casualty from sexual harassment. Little is written about the
effects of sexual harassment on the organization. The authors report on the scant literature found that relate to this issue. To
summarize, the effects sexual harassment has had on organizations have been invisible and are more in tune with financial aspects, namely the costs of absenteeism and turnover.

Koen, Clifford M. "Sexual Harassment Claims Stem from a Hostile Work Environment." *Personnel Journal* 69 (1990): 88-99.

This article gives a historical look at sexual harassment laws
using examples from landmark cases such as Meritor Savings Bank
v. Vinson, Broderick v. Ruder, and Rabidue v. Osceola Refining
Company. What these and other cases point out is that the best
way to avoid liability for sexual harassment is to prevent it from
happening in the first place.

MacKinnon, Catherine. *Sexual Harassment of Working Women.* New
Haven, CT: Yale University Press, 1978. 312pp.

MacKinnon, a Yale professor, wrote this book before there
were guidelines and regulations defining sexual harassment. Ar-
guing that sexual harassment was solely a woman's problem, she
views sexual harassment as sexual discrimination. MacKinnon's
arguments are strong, and even though it has been found that men
are also victims of sexual harassment, she paved the way for
making the workplace a safer environment.

Manley, Will. "Sexual Harassment by Patrons." *American Libraries*
24 (October 1993): 828.

This article takes a "potshot" at the increasing problem of
sexual harassment by library patrons. If you read between the

lines of this article, this is an issue that many libraries are finding themselves dealing with. Follow-up articles on this topic appear in succeeding issues of *American Libraries*.

Neugarten, Dail Ann and Jay M. Shafritz. *Sexuality in Organizations: Romantic and Coercive Behaviors at Work*. Oak Park, IL: Moore Publishing, 1980. 166pp.

Even though this book is almost twenty years old, the contents are still valid, and it contains references that give not only a historical perspective, but also a more sound foundation for understanding the impact sexual harassment has on the working population. The book is divided into four sections, each consisting of chapters on issues related to the section. The chapters are all reprints of articles in either scholarly journals or books. There is also a very good article from the *Michigan Law Review* by Alan Goldberg on sexual harassment and Title VII of the Civil Rights Act of 1964.

Paetzold, Ramona L. and Anne M. O'Leary-Kelly. "Continuing Violations and Hostile Environment Sexual Harassment: When is Enough, Enough?" *American Business Law Journal* 31 (1993): 365-395.

This article is an excellent treatise on sexual harassment. It is authoritative and provides a very good historical look at Title VII of the Civil Rights Act of 1964 and subsequent court cases.

— — — . "Hostile Environment Sexual Harassment in the United States: Post Meritor Developments and Implications." *Gender, Work and Organization* 1 (January 1994): 50-57.

The most famous sexual harassment case is Meritor Savings Bank v. Vinson. This article reviews the climate surrounding sexual harassment in the workplace eight years after the verdict. Citing the Clarence Thomas hearings and the Tailhook investigation, the authors delve into liability issues as invoked by Title VII of the Civil Rights Act of 1964. Since Meritor, the courts have held that the plaintiffs can not have invited or incited the behaviors they are complaining about. Generally, the plaintiff also must prove that the harassment resulted because of his or her sex. However, more recently the courts have taken a more general interpretation and have said that conduct, even though not explicitly sensual, can also qualify as sexually harassing.

Petrocelli, Williams and Barbara Kate Repa. *Sexual Harassment on the Job.* Berkeley, CA: Nalo Press, 1992. n.p.

This is a very comprehensive book that describes what sexual harassment is, the laws pertaining to harassment, and how to curtail harassment in the workplace. The authors also have included a list of organizations that are advocates for wronged individuals. Key dates indicating when sexual harassment laws went into effect, common-law tort actions, legal remedies, and workplace policies and programs are covered. It is interesting to note that 70% of all male and female workers have either dated or married someone they met in the workplace. That statistic confuses the issue of sexual harassment in the workplace. The key is that the advances must be unwanted, non-mutual, and unacceptable conduct.

Philipose, Liz. "The Laws of War and Women's Human Rights." *Hypatia 11* (September 1, 1996): 46.

This article is one from an entire issue of *Hypatia* that is devoted to women and violence. It gives an excellent, brief overview of the crimes that have been committed against women. Gender-based violence has long been targeted as a denial of women's human rights.

Rubenstein, M. "Research Awareness Raising Training and Advisory Services to Combat Sexual Harassment." *Conditions of Work Digest* 11 (1992): 285-290.

Sexual harassment in the workplace knows no boundaries and is a real problem for both men and women. This article presents research findings from eight countries, including the United States, and proceeds to explore awareness-raising activities that have taken place in each of these countries. Sexual harassment is perceived as being a definite problem in each of the countries studied. Sexual harassment ranges from gestures and glances to unwanted touching and sexual intercourse. A deterrent to sexual harassment is the establishment of a campaign to bring awareness of the issue. Examples of these campaigns include brochures, leaflets, and films. Training programs on sexual harassment are also an effective awareness-raising activities.

Sheffey, S. and R.S. Tinsdale. "Perceptions of Sexual Harassment in the Workplace." *Journal of Applied Social Psychology* 22 (1992): 1502-1520.

What defines sexual harassment is a complex and confusing matter and there are several definitions throughout the literature. This article considers the various definitions of sexual harassment and goes on to look at assumptions that were derived from a sex-role model developed in 1982.

Shuman, Bruce. "Cheaper than the Holiday Inn: Sex in the Public Library." *Library & Archival Security* 13 (1995): 47-60.

Unwanted sexual behavior can occur in any library. Shuman presents an interesting discussion of these problems and gives countermeasures, as well as legal concerns. The best deterrent is to maintain a well-staffed security force and do not allow loitering, especially near or in the restrooms.

Silverman, Dierdre. "Sexual Harassment: Working Women's Dilemma." *Quest: A Feminist Quarterly* 3 (1976): 15-24.

Meritor Savings Bank v. Vinson was not even hinted at when this article was written. However, the issues are the same. Sexual harassment happens to women of all ages and all occupational groups. Citing statistics from a survey conducted by Working Women United, Silverman reports that 70% of the respondents had experienced at least one instance of sexual harassment on the job and 91% saw harassment as a serious problem. Another 78% said they were angry after experiencing the harassment, and 23% felt frightened. Even though the greater majority of the women were angry and upset, only 25% complained.

Stockdale, Margaret, ed. *Sexual Harassment in the Workplace: Perspectives, Frontiers, and Response Strategies.* Thousand Oaks, CA: Sage, 1996. 303pp.

This monograph is volume five of the *Women and Work* series, and looks at all aspects of sexual harassment. It consists of thirteen chapters, each dealing with a special issue of harassment in academia: women of color, sexual harassment as a moral issue, sexual harassment as a cause of a hostile environment, and the outcomes of sexual harassment. Each chapter is well researched and defined.

Tinsley, H.E.A. and M.S. Stockdale. "Sexual Harassment in the Workplace." *Journal of Vocational Behavior* 42 (1993): 1-4.

Why is sexual harassment so widespread when there is so much publicity about how morally and ethically reprehensible it is? To many, it seems that only a few "scuzzy oafs" do it. Others make sexual harassment possible simply by ignoring it. Tinsley and Stockdale point to various citations to illustrate their arguments. Numerous factors associated with the tendency to harass have come under scrutiny. Some of these factors include gender differences, occupational level, ethnic background, and economic class.

2. WELLNESS ISSUES

Stress

Stress factors have been linked to a wide variety of mental and physical disorders. Doesn't it seem odd, though, to talk about stress-related issues and libraries in the same sentence? Although the two don't appear to have a connection, all one needs to do is talk to a group of librarians to find out that stress and burnout are viable concerns in the profession (Bunge, 1987). In general, work related stress is a fast-growing concern in many organizations. Some of the factors influencing job-related stress include organizational climate, quality of relationships with management and supervisors, job security, quality of physical environment, and clarity of roles. To combat stress symptoms, some organizations offer yoga, meditation, and tai chi (Armour, 1997). Others promote involvement in either physical or mental activity, in addition to offering in-house programs on relieving stress, and on time management techniques (Bold, 1982).

Many researchers recognize the need for some stress in one's life. It provides motivation and challenge and can even improve job performance to some degree (Schneider, 1991). However, too much stress can be detrimental to one's physical and psychological health and job performance. Grosser came up with a model for organizations to follow when dealing with stress:

- consider changing *organizational* characteristics such as policies and procedures
- look at changing *role* characteristics such as reducing workload
- consider job redesign (Grosser, 1985).

Ergonomics

A different type of stress disorder that plagues many businesses, especially libraries, is repetitive motion or stress injuries (RMIs/RSIs). Also called cumulative trauma disorders (CTDs), they can have a debilitating effect on the individual. These injuries aren't new. In fact, they have been documented for hundreds of years, but only for the past ten years has the workplace taken an active role in studying them. The library profession has changed dramatically over the past twenty years. No longer do we pick up the phone and dial a number; instead we type in an E-mail address and message, click, and send. No longer do we use a manual typewriter to type catalog cards; instead we use a computer. In fact, nearly every task librarians do involves a computer. However, improper placement of computer workstations in relation to the user's body has caused physical problems. In fact, the National Institute of Safety and Health (NIOSH) predicts that by the year 2000, 50% of the workforce will suffer from RSI. In 1993 alone, employers spent more than $20.3 billion on 2.73 million workers' compensation claims due to RSI (Scully, 1997).

Some risks associated with incorrect posture or incorrect placement of the workstation being used are:

- bending wrists too much puts excessive pressure on the median nerve and can inhibit nerve condition and lead to injuries
- resting wrists on the keyboard or table edge creates pressure points that can lead to injury of the median nerves
- if your back is slumped, shoulders hunched, and feet are not flat on the floor or supported by a foot rest, pressure can be created in the lower backs
- if the elbows are bent too much, the circulation to the forearm, the hand, and the fingers is decreased
- if the elbows aren't bent enough, strain on the lower back can result
- sitting too close to the monitor causes eye strain
- eye fatigue, headaches, and eye strain can result from staring at the monitor for long periods of time

Symptoms of repetitive motion/stress injury or computer vision syndrome include:

- tightness, discomfort, stiffness, and pain in the hands, wrists, fingers, forearms, or elbows
- tingling, coldness, or numbness in the hands
- clumsiness or loss of strength and coordination of hands
- pain that wakes you up at night

- feeling a need to massage your hands, wrists, and arms
- tired, achy, itchy, or red eyes
- aches and soreness in the lower back

What can be done about it? Ergonomics, the adjusting of the job to the body or the study and practice of designing a person's work environment to ensure his or her health, safety, and improved job performance, should become a standard in any office. Carpal tunnel syndrome, tendonitis, back strain, eyestrain, and neck and shoulder disorders are all RSIs that can be prevented and alleviated by implementing a simple ergonomics program.

There are several different ways an ergonomic program can be implemented. The best and most direct is to contract with a physical or occupational therapist certified or versed in ergonomic principles to present an educational seminar on CTDs/RSIs and their prevention. As a follow-up and as a method to keep the impetus in place, appoint an ergonomic training team who receives training and has the responsibility to ensure the safety and wellness of staff by giving periodic workshops.

What is proper posture and workstation design? Taking a simplistic approach, the body should be in a neutral position (Lang, 1995). Make sure the workstation and the chair are adjustable and the monitor is positioned 18-29 inches away from the body and at a 15 to 30 degree angle. The mouse should be at the same height and at the side of the keyboard. Continued monitoring of workstations, taking frequent breaks, varying tasks, and reinforcing the importance of ergonomics will help alleviate and prevent RSIs.

Indoor Air Quality

Sick building syndrome has become a frequently mentioned phrase in many libraries and offices, but defining sick building syndrome is a bit difficult because there is no regulatory definition for it. In 1995, the U.S. General Accounting Office released a survey that showed that half of all American schools have problems that affect indoor air quality. Among these problems are poor ventilation, synthetic construction materials, and tightly sealed buildings (Gutman, 1997). Health symptoms are variable and are split into three categories:

- A radical reaction in which a number of people clearly and suddenly become ill. This usually involves limited air exchange combined with something like a chemical cleaner.

- An unhealthy atmosphere, or when many people experience ongoing subtle illness or discomfort. The most common symptoms are sore eyes, sore throat or nasal membranes, low-grade headaches, feeling of lethargy, and higher incidence of upper-respiratory infection.

- A hypersensitive reaction or multiple chemical reaction, when one or more people become very ill. This normally is a result of exposure to chemicals that cause a sensitive reaction (Bomier, 1997).

There are several avenues of action that administration can take when investigating sick building syndrome. A pro-active approach seems to work the best and involves a limited amount of basic testing of the air to determine what kinds of microbes are living in the building. A review of the building air-handling unit and mechanical engineering system should also be documented. Finally, a reliable epidemiological study of comparative absenteeism should be documented (Bomier, 1997). Prevention is the best defense against sick building syndrome.

Summary

The literature covering stress, ergonomics, and indoor air quality concerns is over abundant. The citations shown below give a wide perspective of wellness concerns found in libraries.

Citations

Stress

Armour, Stephanie. "Employers Helping Employees Ease Stress." *Gannett News Service* (March 5, 1998): S12.

Work-related stress is a fast-growing concern among many organizations. To ease employee stress, some firms are offering yoga, meditation, and tai chi. Stress relievers often come in two forms: physical activity and mental relaxation. Armour continues to state that stress is determined by how much control employees have over their jobs, the less the control, the more the stress. Stress is not an inexpensive disorder. It's estimated that $200 billion dollars a year is spent on reduced productivity due to stress.

Arnetz, Bengt B., Mats Berg, and Judith Arnetz. "Mental Strain and Physical Symptoms among Employees in Modern Offices." *Archives of Environmental Health* 5 (January 1997): 63-65.

One would think that working in a new building would be the best job. Researchers are finding this to be far from the truth because there has been an increase in the reported episodes of complaints and symptoms from employees who work in modern buildings. The usual complaints include headache and fatigue.

Bold, Rudolph. "Librarian Burn-Out." *Library Journal* 107 (November 1, 1982): 2048-2051.

What could be stressful about being a librarian? As ironic as it sounds, there is a lot of stress associated with working in a library. Budget reductions, workload, and potential workplace violence all have an impact on library staff. Bold looks at stress symptoms or burn out. Diagnosis of burn out isn't easy, but there are several tests that can be given to pinpoint stress symptoms. To combat stress and burn out, libraries are offering in-house programs and are promoting external or private workshops that focus on methods of relieving stress. Don't let the fact that this article is nearly twenty years old bother you — it is still pertinent to today's library staff.

Brott, Armin A. "New Approaches to Job Stress." *Nation's Business* 82 (May 1, 1994): 81-82.

Job-related stress has been around as long as jobs have. Recognizing the increase in job-related stress, management has begun fitness programs and started encouraging employees to seek counseling for stress-caused problems. Two methods of decreasing stress are to improve communication and increase employees' personal power. Make sure people know what is going on, and keep them involved. However, this involvement shouldn't end at 5:00 p.m. Instead, make sure there are opportunities for employees to enjoy recreation together and celebrate their work successes.

Bube, Judith Lynn. "Stress in the Library Environment." *Technicalities* 5 (July 1985): 7-11.

Bube takes a thorough look at stress and how it affects library employees. She remarks that how one copes with stress can be determined by the resources that are available, one's religious beliefs, one's problem-solving skills, and one's general health and energy.

Bunge, Charles. "Stress in the Library." *Library Journal* 112 (September 15, 1987): 48-51.

This article explores the part stress plays in librarians' work. Some sources of stress are patrons, workload, schedules, lack of positive feedback, technology and equipment, unchallenging work, and change. High on the list are patrons, while change and lack of budget and resources are low on the list. Interestingly, Bunge compares sources of stress of public service and technical service librarians. As can be imagined, public service librarians cite patrons as the number one source of stress, while workload is the number one source of stress among technical service librarians. Support staff cite supervisors and management as their number one source of stress.

——— "Stress in the Library Workplace." *Library Trends* 38 (Summer 1989): 92-102.

This article, written two years after the above article, points out that stress is not uncommon in the library environment; however, stress doesn't have to remain a part of the work environment.

Cherniss, Cary. *Professional Burn Out in Human Services.* New York: Praeger, 1980. 295pp.

This book raises very important issues that were pertinent in 1980 and are still primary concerns for all kinds of professionals, nearly twenty years later. Specifically, Cherniss describes and analyzes what happens to people when they become a professional. Cherniss covers every issue relating to stress and burn-out. This is an excellent book for anyone to read.

Fimian, Michael J., Sandra A. Benedict, and Stacie Johnson. "The Measure of Occupational Stress and Burnout Among Library Media Specialists." *Library & Information Science Research* 11 (January 1989): 3-19.

The authors detail the development of the Media Specialist Stress Inventory (MSSI). Data from 337 media specialists was analyzed and reported. It was concluded that management skills should be developed and staff should be taught how to assess and identify levels of stress sources.

Fisher, David P. "Are Librarians Burning Out?" *Journal of Librarianship* 22 (October 1990): 216-235.

This article gives a thorough look at the problem of stress in the library profession. A ten-year period, 1980-1990, is concentrated on. Emphasis is placed on British libraries.

Grosser, Kerry. "Stress and Stress Management: A Literature Review, Part III." *LASIE* 16 (July/August 1985): 2-23.

In the third part of a three-part series on stress and stress management, Grosser cites some excellent articles that look at an organization's responsibility to its employees when dealing with stress.

McKee, Ken. "The Back Page: Stress? What Stress?" *Texas Library Journal* 72 (Summer 1996): 103-104.

McKee has written a humorous, tongue-in-cheek article on librarians and stress factors. This gives a light hearted view of a serious problem.

Nawe, Julita. "Work-Related Stress Among the Library and Information Workforce." *Library Review* 44 (1995): 30-37.

Work-related stress is a common occurrence in many professions. The author notes that ironically, the major sources of both satisfaction and stress for librarians are the same — patrons and the librarian's colleagues. Nawe concludes that continual development of one's awareness of stress management techniques is important.

Ollendorff, Monica. "How Much Do Librarians Know About Stress Management?" *Behavioral & Social Sciences Librarian* 8 (1989): 67-99.

This article is a study that attempts to determine how much librarians know about stress management and how they handle stress. The author sent out a survey that determined that eighty-two percent of responding librarians think it would be beneficial to learn about stress management techniques. But, sixty percent don't think that stress management is a necessary part of librarianship training. A copy of the survey is included.

Ostler, Larry J. and Jin Teik Oon. "Stress Analysis: A Case Study." *C&RL News* 7 (July 1989): 587-590.

Ostler and Oon have conducted a very thorough examination of the effects of stress in libraries. They report that the four most common sources of stress in libraries are workload, technology, change, and failure.

Roose, Tina. "Stress at the Reference Desk." *Library Journal* 114 (September 1, 1989): 166-167.

In this article, Roose studies the effect stress has on conducting online searches. Citing a 1988 study by Janice Helen McCue, Roose contends that librarians who perform online searches in a separate location do higher quality searches than those who are interrupted. Roose continues and discusses burnout and other psychological syndromes that can be precipitated by stress.

Schneider, Margaret S. "Stress and Job Satisfaction among Employees in a Public Library System with a Focus on Public Services." *Library & Information Science Research* 13 (October/December 1991): 385-404.

Organizational climate has been shown to have an important influence on occupational stress in libraries. Schneider cites a survey done in 1988 of more than 200 employees of a large, urban, public library system. The survey consisted of interviews and a questionnaire and compared public service and technical service employees. Interestingly, although both groups rated their interactions with supervisors and management as positive, public service staff relationships were more positive than those of technical service staff.

Steele, Anitra T. "Read Two Books and Call Me in the Morning." *Wilson Library Bulletin* 68 (June 1994): 65-66.

Be prepared. That is the motto that public libraries need to have in order to handle crises and disasters without getting too stressed-out. This article takes the interesting approach that it isn't always just the staff who get stressed while at work; patrons, even children, can become stressed, so it is important that children's librarians realize this and include items in their collection that deal with stress in children.

Switzer, Teri R. "The Crisis Was Bad, but the Stress Is Killing Me!" *Colorado Libraries* 24 (Fall 1998): 19-21.

After suffering from a rare and devastating disaster, the Colorado State University Libraries was closed for four weeks, yet continued to offer full service to the university, the community, and the state. Switzer describes some of the stress-related issues that the staff dealt with and how the library administration changed policies and procedures to lessen the stress of keeping the status quo when the status quo doesn't exist.

Ergonomics

Anshel, Jeffrey. "Computer Vision Syndrome: Causes and Cures." *Managing Office Technology* 42 (July 1997): 17-19.

Computer operators report more eye-related problems than other office workers who do not use a visual display terminal (VDT). In fact, visual problems occur in 75-90% of all VDT users. Some symptoms of computer vision syndrome are eyestrain, blurred vision, dry and irritated eyes, backache, and double vision.

Atencio, Rosemarie. "Eyestrain: The Number One Complaint of Computer Users." *Computers in Libraries* 16 (1996): 40-43.

Eyestrain has become the most common problem among employees using computers. Atencio lists several preventive measures relating to monitors and lighting.

Balas, Janet. "Library Ergonomics: Serving Special Needs." *Computers in Libraries* 16 (1996): 32-34.

Disabled patrons have ergonomic needs that are somewhat different from those of able-bodied staff. Balas offers online resources that discuss the Americans with Disabilities Act, and suggests modifications to be made to computer workstations.

———. "Making Libraries Comfortable." *Computers in Libraries* (September 1997): 49-50.

Balas, a frequent contributor of ergonomics, and computer-related articles in several journals, suggests that people who want to learn more about ergonomics should consult the ErgoLib web site. The University of Texas at Austin also has a web site that is maintained by its General Libraries Ergonomics Task Force. For those surfers who want to chat, the Ergo Forum site holds online conferences about ergonomic topics every Wednesday evening.

Bencievenga, Dominic. "The Economics of Ergonomics: Finding the Right Fit." *HR Magazine* 41 (August 1, 1996): 68-75.

This article is an excellent overview of the complete ergonomic picture. Repetitive stress injuries (RSIs), indoor air quality, training, and architectural designs are touched on. A short, related article follows this one that gives several ergonomic tips, such as task lighting makes it easier to read printed materials and glare screens help protect eyes from monitor glare.

Bruening, John C. "Standing at the Ready: Charting an Ergonomics Compliance Course." *Managing Office Technology* 42 (November 1997): 20-23.

The Occupational Safety and Health Administration (OSHA) has been trying in vain to get ergonomic standards in force; however, they are not going to give up. Even though there are no specific standards on ergonomics, under section 5a.1 of the OSHA General Duty Clause, employers have an obligation to maintain a workplace that is free of recognized hazards. There are several legislators and employers who question OSHA's role in workplace ergonomics.

Butler, Sharon J. "Common-Sense Ergonomics (Or, What You Don't Do Can Hurt You)." *Computers in Libraries* 17 (September 1997): 35-37.

The library science discipline has changed considerably, and as technology takes its place in libraries, the way librarians do work will continue to change. Butler details thirteen easy steps that can be followed in order to make a person's experience on the job more comfortable: sit up straight, stand straight, position your body properly in front of your computer workstation, don't pound on the computer keys, position your mouse so your arm and shoulder maintain neutral positions, avoid reclining in your chair, avoid resting your arms on the armrests, handle writing tools gently, allow your upper body to move naturally, avoid holding the phone between your head and your shoulder, change your activities periodically, avoid strain when lifting, moving, or carrying books, and listen to your body tell you what hurts and what feels good.

Carpal Tunnel Syndrome, Selected References. Cincinnati, OH: United States Department of Health and Human Services, Centers for Disease Control and Prevention, 1989. n.p.

This compilation of articles on carpal tunnel syndrome was put together in response to the increasing requests for information on RSIs. All the articles describe the results of research conducted or funded by the National Institute of Safety and Health (NIOSH). Although this article is nearly ten years old, the information is still pertinent and useful today.

Chadbourne, Robert D. "Ergonomics and the Electronic Workplace." *Wilson Library Bulletin* 69 (January 1995): 24-26.

Computer injuries come with a large price tag. The average price for carpal tunnel surgery adds up to $2,600, plus the cost of a day in the hospital, recuperation time, and physical therapy for up to six weeks. By paying more attention to the concept called ergonomics, libraries can lessen the harmful effects of computers and the electronic workplace. Chadbourne lists six considerations that are critical to the electronic workplace. These are keyboard height, eye-to-screen distance, viewing angle, hand-to-keyboard distance, seat height, and back support. VDT users also need to take more breaks in order to give their eyes a rest. These breaks, however, don't have to be non-productive ones. Instead, the staff member could go to the circulation desk or do some shelving.

Crouch, Tammy and Michael Madden. *Carpal Tunnel Syndrome and Overuse Injuries.* Berkeley, CA: North Atlantic Books, 1992. n.p.

Holistic medicine, chiropractic care, and alternative therapy for cumulative trauma disorders (CTDs)are the focus.

DeLong, Suzanne. "Don't Stick Your Neck Out, Librarian." *American Libraries* 26 (1995): 694-695.

As a physical therapist, DeLong knows firsthand about the problems that incorrect posture can cause and the activities that librarians perform that contribute to injuries. Many of the tasks that librarians perform require the head to be placed forward at an unnatural angle; therefore, there is a greater risk for neck injury. DeLong offers advice on what to do to prevent neck injuries.

Dieterich, Robert S. "Tunnel Vision." *Computerworld* (March 3, 1995): 77.

This article is an overview of the rising incidents of CTDs. Using data supplied by Tom Cosentino, a health and safety manager at Hoechst Celanese Corporation, the author convincingly presents a series of case studies that will make a believer in ergonomics out of anyone. One of the important ergonomic considerations that Dieterich mentions is the implementation of Windows on computers, because it requires the use of a mouse. Because keyboard trays don't have room to accommodate a mouse, it is usually placed far to the side or above the keyboard, forcing the user to reach. This causes arm and shoulder pain.

Fine, Doug. "A Break Now Saves Money Later; Ergonomics Should be Taken Seriously." *InfoWorld* 17 (May 1995): 54.

RSIs can be harmful to both the employee and the employer. Productivity is seriously hampered when staff are out due to RSIs. Fine briefly discusses ergonomic devices and the proper arrangement of one's workstation.

— — —. "Hands-on Guide to No-pain Computing." *PC World* 14 (June 1996): 149-155.
To make an ergonomic program successful, the employee has to take the matter into his or her own hands. Fine shows the proper placement of the wrists and hands when using a computer.

Fisher, Sandra L. "Are Your Employees Working Ergosmart?" *Personnel Journal* 75 (December 1996): 91-92.
Employees have to be educated in the principles of ergonomics in order for the employer to recognize a decrease in workers' compensation premiums. Fisher illustrates the proper setup of a computer workstation for maximum productivity, while taking into consideration proper ergonomic placement.

Fryer, Bronwyn and Ellen Ignatius. "The High Cost of Keyboard Injuries." *PC World* 12 (March 1994): 45-46.
After realizing a dramatic increase in RSIs in her company, Ignatius took steps to initiate an ergonomic training program.

Labar, Gregg. "Ergonomics for the Virtual Office." *Managing Office Technology* 42 (October 1997): 22-24.
Technology has made it possible to perform one's office duties anywhere at any time. Laptop computers are very popular among traveling staff; however, it is important to consider the ergonomics of laptop computer use. How do users transport them? How do they position them when using them? Labar cautions that one should consider the weight of the laptop. The battery pack, papers, and disks can all add up to seventy pounds, not an insignificant amount of weight.

Lang, Susan S. "Carpal Tunnel Syndrome Protection." *Computers in Libraries* 15 (February 1995): 10, 12.
Cornell University (New York) has conducted a considerable amount of research on carpal tunnel syndrome, and in conjunction with that research, it has been looking at the positioning of keyboards. Its findings showed that a pre-set, tiltdown keyboard kept hands in a neutral position 67% of the time, compared with 42% with traditional keyboards.

"Leading Public Health Scientists Urge Congress to Allow OSHA to Develop Safe Workplace Standard." *U.S. Newservice* (July 11, 1997). Wire service.

More and more organizations, citizens, and community lawmakers are pressing Congress to institute workplace standards. There are more than 750,000 chronic musculoskeletal disorders and over-exertion injuries in United States businesses. These represent one-third of all lost time workplace injuries and cost around a billion dollars each year. There is scientific evidence that a cause-and-effect relationship exists between poor ergonomics in the workplace and chronic musculoskeletal disorders.

Lee, N. N. Swanson, S. Sauter, R. Wickstrom, A. Walker, and M. Mangum. "A Review of Physical Exercises Recommended for VDT Operators." *Applied Ergonomics* 23 (December 1992): 387-408.

If you want some exercises to do to relieve stress from working on a computer, then you need to read this article. The name of each exercise is given, along with the instructions, the muscle groups worked, the anatomical structures stretched, what equipment is needed, how much time is involved, and the level of difficulty. A few diagrams are included.

McClure, Laura. "Thinking Ergonomics." *The Progressive* 58 (August 1994): 40.

Some employers do not recognize the importance of ergonomics as a method for keeping staff healthy and productive. This article describes one employee's experience with her government employer and the indifference to her RSI.

Miller, Kathy. "Ergonomic Products on Parade." *Computers in Libraries* 16 (1996): 44-47.

Miller covers software and kit products that train employees on how to prevent RSIs. Also given are web sites and products that address specific ergonomic injuries.

Neuborne, Ellen. "RSI Workers in Pain; Employers Up in Arms." *USA Today* (January 9, 1997): 01B.

Neuborne reports on a two-day conference on RSIs and their prevention. RSIs cost employers more than $20 billion each year in workers' compensation claims. The government estimates that an additional $80 billion is lost in related costs such as absenteeism and reduced productivity. The author also describes California's new ergonomic law.

Pascarelli, Emil and Deborah Quilter. *Repetitive Strain Injury: A Computer User's Guide.* New York: John Wiley & Sons, 1994. 218pp.
    The authors describe an easy, seven-point plan for preventing RSIs.

Pasher, Victoria Sonshine. "Videos, CD-ROMs Aid Ergonomic Training." *National Underwriter* 101 (1997): 57, 59.
    Pain and cost are two words associated with RMIs. Responding to the prevalence and the cost of these injuries, some insurance companies have developed videos and CD-ROMs to provide ergonomic training and workstation evaluations.

Petersen, Debbie. "Ergonomics 101." *American Printer* 217 (September 1996): 36-39.
    Don't let the journal this article is in fool you. There are several important points made that are very relevant to libraries. The most relevant one concerns lifting standards. According to NIOSH, 51 pounds is the maximum weight workers can handle, if they lift objects properly. Think about boxes of books. Very easily, a box of books could weigh 40 to 50 pounds. Petersen continues to explain the variables that can have negative effects on your back. These are how often you lift, the lateral motion of the spine, how fast you twist, and how far forward you bend.

Peterson, Baird and Richard Patten. *The Ergonomic PC.* New York: McGraw-Hill, 1995. 304 pp.
    This book explains CTDs in detail by means of illustrations and photos. It is an excellent resource for managers and employees.

Pinsky, Mark. *The Carpal Tunnel Syndrome Book.* New York: Warner Books, Inc., 1993. 207pp.
    This is another good resource book on RSIs. Experts give suggestions on how to prevent RSIs in the ten most high-risk occupations.

Robertson, Michelle M. "Ergonomic Considerations for the Human Environment." *School Library Media Quarterly* 20 (1992): 211-215.

Temperature, humidity, noise, and lighting are discussed in this article about the work environment. Robertson lists the correct features that should be considered when designing a workstation.

Romano, Catherine. "Working Out the Kinks." *Management Review* 85 (February 1996): 24-28.

OSHA data reveals that 302,000 upper extremity CTDs (mainly shoulder tendonitis and carpal tunnel syndrome) were reported in 1993. In 1983, this number was only 22,700. Companies need to approach ergonomics on an individual basis, and you can't just give an employee an adjustable chair and leave. Romano describes L.L. Bean's ergonomic program and programs of other well-known corporations.

Scully, Michael. "Insurance: Adjust That Chair! Brighten That Monitor!" *Your Company* (October 1, 1997): 72.

Short and to the point, that's what this article is. Noting that RSIs drive up workers' compensation premiums, the author advises offices to pay attention to employees who complain about stress injuries. Second, he suggests using safety manuals that address RSIs, and, third, warnings about RSIs should be posted on office bulletin boards. Scully continues his case by citing California's law that requires businesses to make their offices ergonomically safer.

Schlisserman, Cortney. "Where to Find Ergonomic Advice." *PC World* 15 (February 1997): 64.

This article is an excellent one if you want to find some ergonomic web sites to visit.

Switzer, Teri R. "An Ounce of Prevention." *C&RL News* 56 (May 1995): 314-317.

RMIs are increasing dramatically. Libraries are particularly affected due to the repetitive nature of the work: the shelving of books and computer use. Switzer gives information about Colorado State University Libraries' five-year ergonomic plan.

Summer, Susan Cook. "Ergonomics Programs and Activities in Research Libraries." *LRTS* 40 (1995): 84-92.

After interviewing 104 heads of technical services departments, Summer compiled the comments and determined that library administrators realize there are problems associated with

RMIs and that most have formed committees to address the issues.

Tannenhous, Norra. *Relief from Carpal Tunnel Syndrome and Other Repetitive Motion Disorders.* New York: Dell Publishing, 1991. 118pp.

This is a very practical guide for assessment of ergonomic safety in the workplace. It is written for the employee, rather than for management.

Tessler, Franklin N. "Smart Input: How to Choose from the New Generation of Innovative Input Devices." *MacWorld* 13 (May 1996): 98-104.

Input devices, keyboards, and voice-activated systems are discussed. Both the pros and the cons are given.

Thornton, Joyce K. "Battling Carpal Tunnel Syndrome through Ergonomics." *Computers in Libraries* 15 (September 1995): 22.

Recognizing the importance of ergonomics as a deterrent to RMIs, the Texas A & M University Sterling Evans Library established a program to address its incidents of ergonomics-related injuries. Thornton presents a step-by-step guide.

Warner, David. "The Occupational Safety and Health Administration." *Nation's Business* 86 (January 1998): 10.

Warner reports on the bill that was introduced to prohibit OSHA from establishing an ergonomic standard. An amendment to the labor, health and human services and education appropriations measure was signed into law in November 1997 and prohibits OSHA from requiring businesses to modify workplaces and redesign jobs that pose ergonomic hazards.

Weeks, James L., Barry S. Levy, and Gregory R. Wagner. *Preventing Occupational Disease and Injury.* Washington, DC: American Public Health Association, 1991.

Occupational safety in the corporate setting is this book's focus. There are several convincing statistics that back the authors' claims.

Werrell, Marjorie and Zachary J. Koutsandreas. "Ergonomics: A Good Place to Start." *Occupational Hazards* 59 (September 1997): 37-40.

Ergonomics plays an important part in injury prevention. Four common fallacies about ergonomics are: 1) if the design is for an average person, it will work for everyone; 2) employees can adapt easily to any job; 3) if ergonomics is addressed, an employee epidemic will result; and 4) ergonomics is expensive.

Wheeler, Brooke C. "The Ergonomic Mac." *MacUser* 13 (May 1997): 87-89.
Reviews and prices are given for products made to make using your computer more ergonomically friendly. Wrist rests, mice, and keyboard trays are looked at.

Wilkinson, Frances C. and Ruth Krug. "Computer Workstation Design and Assessment." *Technical Services Quarterly* 10 (1993): 43-52.
Computers have become an important part of libraries. Because of the potential injuries associated with the use and prevalence of computers in the library environment, the authors stress the need for workstation assessment. Lighting, terminal placement, the desk and chair, and training of personnel in ergonomics are important.

Winter, Metta. "The Healthy Office." *Human Ecology Forum* 25 (Spring 1997): 16-19.
Libraries, like most offices, are computer-oriented, and with the constant use of computers comes a whole new set of problems. By applying ergonomics, the office can be a healthier place to work. Proper lighting can lessen eyestrain, and the healthiest type of lighting is called lensed, indirect uplighting.

Yassi, Annalee. "Repetitive Strain Injuries." *The Lancet* 349 (March 29, 1997): 943-947.
RSI claims increased three fold between 1986 and 1993. RSI is classified as any injury resulting from awkward postures, repetitive motions, and force. Early diagnosis and treatment are key to reducing these injuries.

Indoor Air Quality

Bomier, Bruce. "Prescribing a Cure." *American School & University* 69 (June 1997): 26-28.
"Helplessness" and "confusion" are two words Bomier uses to describe the issue of sick building syndrome. Bomier offers solid,

practical advice on dealing with a building that exhibits symptoms of being sick.

Bush, Carmel and Halcyon Enssle. "Indoor Air Quality: Planning and Managing Library Buildings." *Advances in Librarianship* 18 (1994): 215-236.

Contamination of indoor air can result from its occupants, outdoor air, or building construction and operations. Bush and Enssle have written a well-researched and thorough article on dealing with air quality issues in libraries.

Corbitt, Jo Anne. "Weighing the Costs of IAQ." *Journal of Property Management* 62 (March/April 1997): 4.

This article takes a look at indoor air quality from a real estate/rental market standpoint. However, it gives some sound advice that management should take to heart.

Gallo, Francis M. "You Can Design a Proactive Indoor Air Quality Program." *Managing Office Technology* 42 (January 1997): 25-28.

People spend up to 90% of their days indoors, and the number and variety of air pollutants that are found in indoor air are increasing. In addition, the environmentally conservative buildings of the 1980s are no longer being prescribed because of the problems the lack of ventilation causes. Taking these issues into consideration, Gallo offers excellent advice on cleaning up office air. This article is technical enough to be believable but is still readable.

Greene, Robert E., John Casey, and Phillip Williams. "A Proactive Approach for Managing Indoor Air Quality." *Journal of Environmental Health* 60 (November 1997): 15-21.

Some of the issues involved in indoor air quality include "psychosocial" issues such as ergonomics, acoustics, and personal sensitivity and social factors. Looking at these concerns and heating, ventilation, and air conditions systems, Greene outlines a plan for addressing indoor air quality problems. Environmental Protection Agency guidelines back his recommendations.

Gutman, Barbara. "Cleaning Up Sick Buildings." *NEA Today* 16 (November 1997): 9.

Gutman wrote her master's thesis on sick building syndrome and its effects on Vermont schools. This article is a short summary of the research she conducted. She recommends forming a committee to analyze and help improve the air quality in schools.

Henderson, Zorika Petic. "Rx for Sick Buildings." *Human Ecology Forum* 23 (June 1995): 17-19.

This article cites Alan Hedge, a professor of design and environmental analysis and an expert on indoor air pollution. Hedge states that indoor air pollution is a complex problem and any building that has problems must be comprehensively analyzed. Henderson cites some interesting findings from a survey conducted at sample sites around the United States.

Odom, J. David and Christine R. Barr. "Sick-building Litigation: The Role that Occupant Outrage Plays." *Journal of Environmental Law & Practice* 4 (May/June 1997): 21-25.

Effective communication can reduce the total cost of sick building syndrome. Addressing emotions and taking early action are both important when investigating indoor air quality problems.

Shideler, Larry. "Filtering out the Facts." *American School & University* 69 (July 1997): 28-29.

Shideler reviews criteria for selecting air filters that are used as a preventive for poor indoor air quality. He outlines a plan of attack and prevention methods.

3. COLLECTION SECURITY

Theft, mutilation, flood, arson, and pests – these are only a few of the perils that befall library collections. There are few libraries that haven't suffered from loss caused by one of these situations. Perhaps one of the most famous library collections is that of the Library of Congress. Security measures at the Library of Congress have been considered a top priority for more than 100 years. In fact, in 1896 Ainsworth Rand Spafford, then librarian of Congress, testified before the Joint Committee on the Library and complained, ". . . in all great libraries, and in many smaller ones, there are continual depredations, cutting from newspapers by unscrupulous readers, attempts to abstract books, and other processes of thieving . . . That is the core in all countries; men of great ability have sometimes been thieves in public libraries" (Billington, 1996).

Theft

Library theft is a problem that seems to be never ending, and regardless of the precautions taken, book thefts seem to take place. Library materials are stolen for a variety of reasons. Sometimes the patron simply keeps the item rather than return it late and other times people steal library materials and sell them to supplement their incomes (Kleberg, 1982). Stephan Blumberg is probably the most notorious thief in the history of library crime. After stealing more than 25,000 items from 300 United States libraries in the early 1990s, Blumberg was finally caught, tried, and convicted.

However, library thefts aren't only committed by outsiders. Statistics reveal that staff commit 25% of all library thefts (Bahr, 1989). Preventing employee theft can be a bit difficult, but with proper applicant screening, it's possible to weed out some people who aren't as trustworthy as they should be. Personal interviews, reference checks, and implementing honesty or core integrity tests can help managers in the hiring process

(Buss, 1993). Some experts maintain that an encouraging and positive work environment can foster positive attitudes towards a company; therefore, employees would be less likely to steal (Buss, 1993).

Interestingly, many libraries don't realize that materials have been taken until they receive a call from an alert book dealer. Several libraries don't conduct inventories of their collections and others don't bother to identify security problems nor do they prosecute book thieves (Goldberg, 1993).

Special and Rare Collections

The security of special or rare collections poses distinct problems. These are so different, in fact, that the Rare Books and Manuscripts Section of the Association of College and Research Libraries of the American Library Association has written security guidelines solely for special collections. Rare books, maps, and other antiquities are appealing to thieves simply because of their worth. The motives for stealing rare books are the same as for other library materials. Some books are stolen by kleptomaniacs; others are stolen to sell for profit. Regardless why people steal library materials, theft of rare books has increased. Some reasons for this include: 1) an increase in the value of rare books; 2) poor internal control and relaxed, user friendly environment; and 3) difficulties protecting special collection items (Chadwick, 1998).

Security measures can be more controlled in special collections than in libraries in general. First, it is wise to conduct a security audit in order to pin point lapses in the present security measures. Next, a security plan should be drafted that delineates acceptable practices in special and rare book collections. Some recommendations to be included in the security plan are:

- require patrons to make appointments to use the materials
- limit the number of people who can use the collections at one time
- prohibit coats, briefcases, and book bags from being carried into the room
- allow only paper, writing instruments, and laptop computers

- don't offer self-service photocopying; instead, have the librarian make the copies
- ensure that staff know the procedures
- set up a reading room so all stations can be easily observed (Trinkaus-Randall, 1998).

Arson

Fires tend to be particularly devastating because not only do they destroy the items they come into contact with, there is also water, foam, soot, and smoke damage. Fortunately, fires in libraries are not common, but they do occur.

There are some basic physical improvements to the building that can be made to help prevent arson. These include reinforcing doors and windows, installing smoke and heat detectors that are connected to the fire or police station, consider moving the book drop to an outside location, and close off in-building book returns from the rest of the building (Morris, 1984).

Collection Preservation

Once library materials have been damaged, they need to be evaluated for restoration. Some materials may be destroyed beyond repair; others may be repaired and returned to the shelves. The preservation of materials is a concern for librarians and archivists. Acid decay, fungus, mildew, and pests adversely affect the condition of collections. Preservation techniques have vastly improved over the past several years. With the advent of the Wei T'o system, water logged items can be dehydrated and brought back to life (Scott, 1988). The use of fungicides and irradiation has made it possible to successfully treat slightly moldy books.

There are several common sense tips recommended to keep collections in good repair:
- regulate temperature and humidity to the recommended ranges of 45-40% humidity and 60 degrees Fahrenheit for book storage
- use air filters to remove dust and gaseous pollutants
- ultraviolet light should be kept at a minimum
- vacuum book stacks on a regular basis
- restrict food in the building which attracts pests (Morris, 1986).

Protecting a library collection from mutilation, theft, arson, and fungus is a necessary and time-consuming project. The selective bibliography that follows is a representative sample of the hundreds of books and journal articles that have been written about collection security and preservation.

Citations

General Collection Security

Abid, Ann B. "Loss Liability: Risk, Responsibility, and Recovery." *Art Documentation* 10 (Winter 1991): 185-187.

Abid expands on a common theme prevalent in collection management discussions, access versus security of the collection. Abid covers insurance, disaster preparedness, and security systems. When talking about security systems, Abid notes that it takes both electronic and human surveillance to ensure the complete safety of the collection. There are three electronic systems that fall under two forms of electrical energy — radio frequency and electromagnetism. Radio frequency systems are less expensive than electromagnetic ones, and are fairly free of false alarms.

Boss, Richard W. "Collection Security." *Library Trends* 33 (Summer/Spring 1984/1985): 39-48.

Libraries tend to react to collection losses, rather than act in a proactive manner. When taking a more pro-active stance against collection loss, library administrators need to define what security is needed. The security shouldn't be limited solely to the collection, but also encompass the physical area. There generally are several weaknesses in a library's security. Boss expands on this idea and outlines eleven areas that tend to be weak.

Lunde, Diane B. "The Disaster at Colorado State University Libraries: Recovery and Restoration of the Collection." *Colorado Libraries*. 24 (Fall 1998): 22-26.

Disaster recovery is Colorado State University Libraries first and middle names. Following a flash flood that swept through campus and destroyed the entire basement of the university, the library has learned what disaster recovery of a collection really is. Lunde offers a first-hand account of what the library has been dealing with and offers several pointers.

O'Neill, Robert K. "Management of Library and Archival Security: From the Outside Looking In." *Journal of Library Administration* 25 (1998).

Edited by O'Neill, this entire issue is devoted to library collection security. Articles covering special collection security, stolen antiquities, preservation, and policies and procedures to protect holdings are included.

Sable, Martin. *The Protection of the Library and Archive: An International Bibliography.* New York: Haworth, 1983. 183 pp.

With an international scope, Sable has brought together the literature of librarianship and archiving. The entries are arranged in broad categories then chronologically. The majority of the entries are periodical articles, but some books, pamphlets, and conference proceedings are included. This is a very complete citation listing of the literature, of which some is pre-1900.

Zeidberg, David S. *Collection Security in ARL Libraries, SPEC Kit 100.* Washington, DC: ARL/OMS, 1984. 102pp.

Responses from a survey sent to the members of the Association of Research Libraries are summarized in this informative publication. It was found that 31% of the responding libraries had security officers, 15% had collection security policies, and 87% were marking their general collections. Security policies and procedures from a wide variety of association libraries are included.

Theft of Materials

Allen, Susan M. "Theft in Libraries and Archives: What to Do During the Aftermath of a Theft." *Journal of Library Administration* 25 (1998): 3-13.

This article is a revision and update of Allen's previous one that appeared in *College and Research Libraries News* in 1990. Allen covers recovery plans, inventory, how to break the news, and possible consequences that may occur. It is interesting to note that the author recognizes that law enforcement personnel often are slow in realizing how serious theft of library materials is. Allen doesn't say anything that hasn't been said before, which is proof that theft of library materials is still happening in the same way, even though more libraries have security systems.

Antwi, I.K. "The Problem of Library Security: The Bauchi Experience." *International Library Review* 21 (July 1989): 363-372.

During a two-month period in 1985, the Abubakar Tafawa Balcwa University Library in Bauchi, Nigeria, experienced a series of book thefts. This article reports the security issues that were unraveled when the thefts were investigated and the measures that were taken to ensure a repeat would not occur. This is a positive article on how one library learned from its mistakes.

Bahr, Alice Harrison. "The Thief In Our Midst." *Library & Archival Security* 9 (1989): 77-81.

Bahr, noted for her research on security issues, uses case studies to prove her point that staff commit nearly one-fourth of all library material thefts.

Behrman, Sara. "When Trust Isn't Enough." *American Libraries* 29 (May 1998): 172-175.

Behrman notes that theft of library materials isn't always committed by outsiders; staff can be, and are, just as guilty of fraud, embezzlement, theft, mutilation of materials, misuse of public funds, and harassment. Some interesting information is that, 90% of the time, insider crime goes undetected; insider crime is often committed by longtime employees for reasons ranging from greed to revenge; and good internal controls need to be enforced in order to curtail insider crime. Behrman uses real-life examples to illustrate how library staff commit crimes.

Billington, James H. "Collections Security: Dr. Billington Tells Congressional Panel of LC Efforts." *Library of Congress Information Bulletin* 54 (December 11, 1995): 479-81.

The Library of Congress is the nation's foremost collector of the printed word. So extensive are its collections that there are some publications that can only be found there. This article is the testimony of the Library of Congress director, Dr. James Billington, to Cngress on the library's efforts to maintain collection security. Billington also includes information about electronic transactions. Over the past three years, the library has taken extensive steps to improve security. There are now guards, alarm gates, and motion detectors.

———. "Here Today, Here Tomorrow: The Imperative of Collections Security." *American Libraries* 27 (August 1996): 40-41.

The Library of Congress is the premier collector of the printed word, and its collections are under constant threat. In 1846, the library spent $1,440 to employ two "watchmen." Today, more than

110 police officers are employed, and over the past six years, $12 million has been spent on new security measures. After several thefts in the early 1990s, the stacks were closed and browsing became a pastime long forgotten. One of the Library of Congress' greatest challenges has been the need to balance access with preservation. Some measures taken include embedding special alarmed targets in 3 million of its books, installing 100 surveillance cameras, limiting the number of items that can be checked out, and installing an automated reader registration system.

Burrows, John and Diane Cooper. *Theft and Loss from UK Libraries: A National Survey.* London: Home Office Police Department, 1992. 56pp.

The authors used both United States and United Kingdom literature to write this short book. Books aren't the only items at risk. Records, cassettes, and other audio-visual materials are also subject to theft. While theft by staff does not account for many problems, it is a concern. The authors also cover reduction of theft by such methods as closed-circuit televisions, security staffing, book tagging, and warning posters.

Buss, Dale. "Ways to Curtail Employee Theft." *Nation's Business* 81 (April 1993): 36-38.

Employee theft has been recognized as a problem for several years. Although this article is not about theft in libraries, it still provides important information for any organization employing people. According to a security consultant, 30% of American workers plan to exploit their employer via theft and another 30% are tempted and may succumb from time to time. This certainly isn't an encouraging statistic. To help prevent this from occurring, the author recommends conducting a thorough applicant screening including personal interviews, credit checks, and reference checks. Another tool to use is an "honesty test" that screens potentially untrustworthy employees. According to some experts, one of the most effective means against employee theft is encouraging a positive attitude towards the organization.

Carson, Charles R. *Managing Employee Honesty.* Los Angeles: Security World Publishing, 1977. 230pp.

The value of this book lies in the case histories and related questions that are given. Each chapter closes with a relevant case history and questions that should be considered. The case histories allow the reader to more fully understand the text and make the text seem to come alive.

Chernofsky, J.L. "Recognizing the Crime of Book Theft." *AB Bookman's Weekly* 90 (July 6, 1992): 3.

This short editorial recognizes the efforts booksellers, librarians, and police have taken to ensure the safety of library materials. By cooperating with one another, it is possible not only to retrieve stolen collections, but also to apprehend the thieves.

Curtis, Bob. *How to Keep Your Employees Honest.* New York: Lebhar-Friedman Books, 1979. 229pp.

Even though this book is a bit dated and focuses on the retail industry, it still has some good tips that we library administrators should use in keeping our staffs honest. Some suggestions given by Curtis include making sure employees know they make worthwhile contributions to the organization, encourage participation in goal setting, open communication lines, and encourage decision making at lower levels.

Dell, S. "Graham John Sanders and the Alexander Turnbull Library." *Archifacts* (April 1992): 30-36.

Dell takes an in-depth look at Sanders' theft of library materials. By enforcing policies and having the right kind of security equipment, the thefts could have been avoided. In addition, staff should be alert and willing to enforce policies.

Flagg, Gordon. "Librarians Meet to Fight Book Thieves." *American Libraries* 14 (November 1983): 648-650.

Libraries need to take pro-active steps to reduce book thefts. Some of these steps include visibly marking library materials, reporting thefts and considering all aspects of having inaccessible stacks.

Goldberg, M. "The Neverending Saga of Library Theft." *Library & Archival Security* 12 (1993): 87-100.

There are very few libraries that regularly take inventories of their collections. There are even fewer that try to identify security problems and fewer still that prosecute thieves. Goldberg studies these issues and notes that some libraries don't think about their own staffs as being culprits and therefore don't take the necessary steps to protect collections from inside pilfering.

Griffith, Jack W. "Library Thefts: A Problem That Won't Go Away." *American Libraries* 9 (April 1978): 224-227.

Regardless of the precautions taken and security systems installed, book thefts will take place. Griffith lists steps that a library should take to reduce the loss of materials strictly due to theft.

Hanff, Peter E. "The Story of the Berkeley Library Theft." *C&RL News* 45 (June 1984): 284-287.

This article is an example of how a skilled thief can pilfer rare books, change the markings, and make them nearly undetectable as stolen. Among some of the lessons learned from the theft was that the bookselling community plays a vital role in identifying and resolving cases of book theft.

Hollinger, Richard D. and John P. Clark. *Theft by Employees.* Lexington, MA: Lexington Books, 1983. 148pp.

This book is for management who seek hard-core research that depicts the increasing plight of employee theft. The research was done in two phases and consisted of face-to-face interviews and mail-in surveys. The data is for a three-year period. Even though the figures are out of date, the research is solid, and it illustrates the pattern and prevalence of employee theft.

Huntsberry, J.S. "The Legacy Theft: The Hunt for Stephan Blumberg." *Art Documentation* 10 (1991): 181-183.

This is a very interesting article describing the detective who finally caught Blumberg after twenty years of theft activity. It gives some important issues to consider. For example, how did Blumberg continue to enter and use special and rare book rooms even though his appearance was questionable? Huntsberry also offers suggestions to deter thefts.

Johansson, David. "Library Material Theft, Mutilation, and Preventive Security Measures." *Public Library Quarterly* 15 (1996): 51-66.

Library budgets do not keep up with inflation. Keeping that in mind, it is becoming more important that libraries provide security for their collections. Johansson focuses on the methods used throughout history to reduce or prevent library material theft and mutilation. This is an excellent source for background information on security measures that have been implemented since A.D. 627.

Kleberg, John R. "A Rx for Library Security." *Library & Archival Security* 4 (1982): 23-30.

This article focuses primarily on theft of library materials. Library materials are usually stolen for one of the following reasons: instead of returning the materials late, some people will just keep them, or some people steal library materials and sell them as a source of income. Good communication between library personnel and security officers and police is essential to an effective library security program. It is important to conduct two surveys: one is an inventory sample, and the other is a survey of the physical facility.

Luurtsema, David. "Dealing with Book Loss in an Academic Library." *Library & Archival Security* 14 (1997): 21-27.

This article uses two scenarios to illustrate how library materials slip through detection systems. The author stresses that an electronic security system will never be able to operate at its full potential in an academic library without staff understanding the procedures and knowing how to implement the policies on theft of materials.

Mosley, Shelley, Anna Caggiano, and John Charles. "The Self Weeding Collection, The Ongoing Problem of Library Theft, and How to Fight Back." *Library Journal* 121 (October 15, 1996): 38-40.

The authors take a good-hearted look at the ongoing problem of library theft. Recognizing that libraries seem to be treated as payment-optional bookstores, they delve into the issues surrounding the problem and list thirty-one preventive measures. The preventive measures are divided into groups: policy, security, design and equipment, collection strategy, and people.

Murphy, Kevin R. *Honesty in the Workplace.* Pacific Grove, CA: Brooks/Cole Publishing Company, 1993. 252pp.

Written by a professor of psychology at Colorado State University, this book discusses why some organizations have loyal, honest employees and why others don't. Murphy discusses how attitudes, organizational climate, trust, and loyalty affect an organization's success. It is well researched, practical, and easy to read.

Nelson, Norman L. "Reducing Theft, Mutilation and Defacement of Library Materials." *Conservation Administration News* 14 (April 1984): 1-4.

How do you reduce theft and mutilation of library materials? Nelson takes a close look at mutilation of materials and offers suggestions for protecting all library materials, including rare books and special collections. Two keys to a good plan are to have the cooperation of the library staff and to make the public aware of the problem.

Onadiran, G.T. "Book Theft in University Libraries in Nigeria." *Library & Archival Security* 8 (Fall/Winter 1988): 37-48.

Theft of library materials knows no boundaries. As the most populous country in Africa, Nigeria is the university home to more than 100,000 students. With a student population that large, the university libraries cannot afford to ignore the potential theft of library materials. However, when survey data is analyzed, it is found that 17% of the respondents reported that book thefts were severe and more than two-thirds of the respondents confessed that they didn't have an inventory system and had never taken inventories of their collections. Some solutions are given, including purchasing multiple copies of textbooks. In the long run, however, this isn't very cost effective.

"No. 1 Concern: Librarian Orders Increased Security Measures for Collections." *Library of Congress Information Bulletin* 54 (October 2, 1995): 413.

As keeper of more than 100 million books, maps, and prints, the Library of Congress has a large responsibility for ensuring the safety of these materials. Some of the steps the Library of Congress has taken to tighten its security include increasing patrols of the stacks, installing of surveillance cameras in the stacks and reading rooms, locking rare books in cages, and handing out special passes for staff who need to have access to the stacks to do their jobs.

Rude, R. and R. Hauptman. "Theft, Dissimulation and Trespass: Some Observations on Security." *Library & Archival Security* 12 (1993): 17-22.

Libraries need to maintain a middle ground between security of and access to materials. The basis for this article is the famous Cheshire case, in which a patron sole more than 15,000 books and piano scores over a twenty-year period from the University of California in Riverside.

"Security of Library Collections." *State Librarian* 38 (July 1991): 26.

This one-page article is a concise overview of security solutions for library buildings, as written by the National Preservation Office at the British Library. Among their building and premises tips are to make sure doors and windows have locks and door hinges are mounted on the inside, install external alarms, and ensure that lighting is adequate. Collection security issues include marking materials with an ownership stamp, electronically tagging materials, storing valuable materials in a secure area, and locking exhibition cases. Staff security solutions include wearing identification badges, not allowing staff to work alone at night or in remote areas, and making sure all staff are properly trained.

Snyder, Neil H., O. Whitfield Broome, Jr., Williams J. Kehoe, James T. McIntyre, Jr., and Karen E. Blair. *Reducing Employee Theft, A Guide to Financial and Organizational Controls.* New York, NY: Quorum Books, 1991. 202pp.

Employee theft can go far beyond the simple home use of office pens, paper clips, tape, and paper. In fact, more than $40 billion worth of goods and property is stolen by employees each year. This book is a compilation of previously published articles on dealing with employee theft. Covered in this book are strategies for reducing theft, ethics, internal controls, security devices, and how to hire and keep quality employees. Included are a very useful appendix and an internal control checklist.

Tomaiuolo, Nicholas. "Deterring Book Theft: Our Common Responsibility." *Wilson Library Bulletin* 63 (January 1989): 58-59.

This article reviews the use of security guards. In general, this isn't the best way to curtail theft because too often the guards will wave students through without properly checking their book bags and briefcases.

Towner, L.W. "An End to Innocence." *American Libraries* 19 (1988): 210-213.

Libraries are allowing themselves to be more vulnerable to theft. Towner puts the blame on librarians who are ignorant, complacent, and neglect to know or enforce the rules.

Dealing with Arson

"Arson Cited in Fresno Blaze." *American Libraries* 25 (January 1994): 17.

This short column describes the fire that damaged the Fresno (California) Public Library.

Fisher, Steve. "The Library Arsonist." *Colorado Libraries.* 24 (Fall 1998): 7-8.

As a member of the University of Denver's library disaster action team, Fisher knows first-hand what happens when a fire breaks out in a library. He offers a personal account of the fire and gives suggestions for administration to follow if faced with a similar situation.

Hubbard, William J., Ronald P. Sasha, and George F. Lord. "Towering Inferno II – Recovering from an Electrical Fire in a Multi-Story Library." *Library & Archival Security* 13 (1995): 61-75.

This article takes an in-depth look at what happened when a fire broke out in the thirteen-story Jacksonville (Florida) State University Library. All facets of the disaster are covered, from evacuation to temporary service and then to restoration of full service.

"Is Your Library Safer from Fire?" *American School and University* 28 (April 1980): 60-63.

Water logged books, black soot everywhere, lost card files — these are some of the issues libraries that have experienced fires contend with. Although fires in libraries are not common, they can occur. Included in this article is a table showing fires that have occurred in North American college and university libraries during a twenty-nine period, 1950-1979. Of those reported, 55% were incendiary, and 50% of those were arson. One needs to take into consideration the time period studied — it includes the restless years of the late 1960s and early 1970s during the Vietnam conflict riots. Some tips to strengthen a library against arson and fires of any kind include improving book drops, providing a fire-resistant cart to use as the receptacle, installing an on/off sprinkler head in the book drop, considering a remote book drop rather than an interior one, strengthening doors, door locks and accessible windows, and lighting up the premises.

Kennedy, John. "Library Arson." *Library Security Newsletter* (September 1976): 1-2.

This short column gives some good advice on how to prevent and combat suspicious fires.

Mathews, Fred W. "Dalhousie Fire." *Canadian Library Journal* 43 (August 1986): 221-226.

Mathews presents details about the recovery efforts following a devastating fire at the law library in the Dalhousie University Weldon Law Building. Included are notes on volunteer training; cleaning, freezing, and vacuum drying of materials and the recovery planning process.

Morris, John. "Los Angeles Library Fire – Learning the Hard Way." *Canadian Library Journal* 44 (March 1987): 217-221.

When the Los Angeles Library was the victim of a fire, more than 375,000 books were destroyed and another 700,000 were wet. Damages were calculated to be $22 million. Morris relates details about the fire and why it spread so quickly.

— — —. *Managing the Library Fire Risk.* Berkeley, CA: University of California Press, 1979. 147pp.

Almost considered a landmark on protecting libraries from fire, Morris' book is full of timeless information. It presents common-sense tips, and even though most of the suggestions are now required by law, it can still serve as a checklist for renovation projects.

— — —. "Protecting the Library from Fire." *Library Trends* 33 (Summer 1984): 49-56.

If one considers the statistic that 30% of all library fires are not incendiary in origin, more care would be taken to ensure that libraries are not targets for arson. Morris studies library fires from 1972 to 1980, and reports that 50% were the results of arson. To help prevent arson and vandalism, some basic physical improvements to the building are needed. These include strengthening doors and windows against intrusion, installing smoke detectors and heat detectors that are attached to a central station alarm system that would alert the fire department, and installing an automatic sprinkler system. Although the information is a bit dated, the tips are worthwhile: review insurance policies to make sure coverage is adequate, insure the collection for replacement value, install intruder detection systems, install outside book drops, and close off in-building book returns from the rest of the library.

Plotnick, Art. "Salvaged Hopes. If It Had to Happen, This Was the Best Time." *American Libraries* 17 (June 1986): 384-386.

The Los Angeles Public Library fire resulted in several million dollars of damage to the building and the contents. Plotnick credits the work of 1,400 volunteers, city firefighters, library staff, and a

$2 million gift from the J. Paul Getty Trust with turning the catastrophe into a more positive event.

St. Lifer, Evan and Michael Rogers. "Arson Strikes CT's Danbury Public Library after Hours." *Library Journal* 121 (April 1, 1996): 14.

Heavy damage was suffered by the Danbury (Connecticut) Public Library when a fire broke out shortly after closing. Books, CDs, and audio-visual materials were damaged in the fire that is said to have resulted in $2 million worth of damage. The fire was started in the book drop.

Trinkley, Michael. *Can You Stand the Heat? A Fire Safety Primer for Libraries, Archives, and Museums.* Atlanta, GA: Southeastern Library Network, 1993. n.p.

Trinkley's paperback book is exactly what its title states, a primer. It contains practical, down-to-earth advice on how to prevent fires and what to do if one occurs.

Mutilation of Materials

Birney, Ann E. and Sara R. Williams. "Mutilation and the Folklore of Academic Librarianship." *Library & Archival Security* 7 (1985): 41-47.

This is an excellent review of the literature published on mutilation and destruction of library materials. The authors also touch on disruptive behavior, but the main focus is on material safety.

Gouke, Mary Noel and Marjorie E. Murfin. "Periodical Mutilation: The Insidious Disease." *Library Journal* 105 (September 1980): 1795-1797.

This article takes an interesting slant on the problem of material mutilation. It studies the prevalence of user education and mechanical security systems as deterrents to mutilation. In fact, user education cut mutilation by 23% and mechanical security systems have been found to reduce mutilation by up to 60%.

Hendrick, Clyde and Marjorie E. Murfin. "Project Library Ripoff: A Study of Periodical Mutilation in a University Library." *College and Research Libraries* 35 (November 1974): 402-411.

Kent State University (Ohio) is focused. A survey was sent to 168 students to determine why they destroy periodicals and what their attitudes towards the library are. As one can imagine, the mutilators had a less favorable impression of the library than those who didn't mutilate materials.

Murfin, Marjorie E. and Clyde Hendrick. "Ripoffs Tell Their Story: Interviews with Mutilators in a University Library." *Journal of American Librarianship* 1 (May 1975): 8-12.

This is a follow-up to the authors' article published in 1974 about the Kent State University (Ohio) survey of students who mutilate library periodicals. This article is interesting because it contains interviews with the students identified in the 1974 study.

"Periodical Mutilation Zooms." *Library Journal* 100 (June 15, 1975): 1172.

As long as there are razor blades, scissors, and human hands, library materials will be vandalized. Even though photocopiers weren't as prevalent when this article was written as they are now, the author notes that the presence of copiers has had no effect on defacement of library materials. Some of the reasons for this mutilation range from laziness to censorship.

Varner, Carroll. "Journal Mutilation in Academic Libraries." *Library & Archival Security* 5 (1983): 19-29.

The University of Nebraska conducted a study of journal mutilation in 1982 that identified four types of mutilators: casual, frustrated, pressured, and selfish.

Weiss, Dana. "Book Theft and Book Mutilation in a Large Urban University Library." *College & Research Libraries* 42 (July 1981): 341-347.

This article reports the results of a study by New York University conducted to determine the motive behind library material mutilation. The results of this study were similar to the one (above) conducted by the University of Nebraska: students are more likely to mutilate materials if they are under pressure for academic success.

Special Collections and Archival Security

Allen, Susan M. "Preventing Theft in Academic Libraries and Special Collections." *Library & Archival Security* 14 (1997): 29-43.

Ever since Stephan Blumberg was tried and convicted for stealing 25,000 titles from 300 United States libraries in the early 1990s, theft of library materials has plagued librarians. During

1993 the number of incidents of library theft increased dramatically. Allen poses pointed questions and then provides the answers — answers that aren't necessarily simple or straightforward. She concludes by stressing that theft is a complicated problem and often a library doesn't even know it has been victimized until the stolen materials are returned. There are some steps that can be taken to curtail theft. These include having a library security officer and library security planning team in place to take regular inventories and make assessments of vulnerable items.

Berger, Sidney. "Special Collections and Security." *Focus on Security* 8 (January 1996): 8-17.

Berger's article examines the vulnerability of special collections and details some measures that can be implemented to provide extra security for the collections. As the author remarks, much of what he presents is pure logic. One of these logical measures is to pay attention to the type of markings that are placed on materials. Some markings are ostentatious; others are eminently visible, and still others are practically invisible. When marking books housed in a rare book room, it is important to know what the scholars want in that book. Some markings are aesthetically placed, while others ruin the endpapers and make the book less valuable.

———. "What is So Rare. . .Issues in Rare Book Librarianship." *Library Trends* 36 (1987): 9-22.

Thefts from rare book collections are increasing. Berger gives some worthwhile tips to follow in order to curtail the loss of rare book materials. Restrict the access to materials, require appropriate user identification, publicize any losses that might occur, prosecute the thieves, work with police to track down items, and mark all materials.

Chadwick, William E. "Special Collections Library Security: An Internal Audit Perspective." *Journal of Library Administration* 25 (1998): 15-31.

White-collar crime has become a serious problem in the United States and has found its way into libraries. Some of the nation's most prestigious universities have been victims of theft from their university archives and rare book collections. Chadwick recommends that management send a message from top to bottom and issue an employee code of conduct and business ethics policy as deterrents to inside theft. Some topics to cover in the policy include conflict of interest, fair competition, copyright laws, software piracy, accounting, gifts and entertainment, confidentiality, fraud, and arm's-length relationships.

Cupp, C.M. *Security Considerations for Archives: Rare Books, Manuscript, and Other Special Collections.* Wright-Patterson Air Force Base, OH: Air Force Institute of Technology, 1989. 21pp.

Even though it is recognized that collections need to be secure and free from theft and mutilation, many times cost inhibits the installation of security measures. Cupp gives some relatively inexpensive methods to employ. These include written policies and procedures covering security of the collection and the building, analyzing different alarms, locks, and surveillance equipment, and has a set of guidelines on how to recover after a disaster.

Everitt, Cynthia A. "Security in Map Collections." *Library Trends* 29 (Winter 1981): 483-498.

Everitt takes a fresh look at maps as holders of vast amounts of information. However, she notes that maps have long been neglected parts of the library collections and even admits that there is little information on map security. To begin, Everitt starts with three assumptions: 1) most security systems don't protect flat maps; 2) many libraries have already tried to prevent map loss; and 3) map security is, in general, neglected. Using these assumptions, the author identifies 230 collections of 50,000 maps and poll opinions, experiences, and reactions to sheet map loss. The majority (68%) of the respondents stated that map loss was a problem and only 8% reported that there even was a problem. It's interesting to note that there are two schools of thought regarding map circulation policies: maps that are allowed to circulate were not as likely to be stolen and a non-circulation policy helps control the collection. Included are the survey and a list of libraries receiving them.

Galvin, T. "The Boston Case of Charles Merrill Mount: The Archivist's Arch Enemy." *American Archivist* 53 (1990): 442-450.

This article describes the rare book thefts of Mount. It is an interesting tale that ends with the author suggesting that the only true method of preventing theft is to institute body searches. However, noting that body searches are constitutionally not allowed, this leaves the reader with the question of whether there really is a foolproof means of preventing theft.

Gandert, Slade Richard. *Protecting Your Collection.* Binghamton, NY: Haworth Press, 1982. 144pp.

Although somewhat outdated, this volume still has valuable advice on keeping rare books, manuscripts, and works of art secure from losses due to theft, fire, flood, and mutilation. This is a reprint of volume four, issues one and two of *Library & Archival Security.*

Hulyk, Barbara R. "Rare and Valuable Documents: Identification, Preservation, and Security Issues." *North Carolina Libraries* 48 (Summer 1990): 118-121.

Frequently, libraries ignore the preservation of important maps, plates and other documents. Hulyk takes a look at what constitutes "rare books" and how some government documents fit in that category. There are several Superintendent of Documents classification numbers that can be designated as "special." These are items in the Z section covering the first Congress. After identifying documents classified as "rare and valuable," the next consideration is to look into conservation and security of these items. Year-round temperature and humidity control is important. Financial resources, space, and staffing all affect the security arrangements in a library.

Lieberman, R. "Security Concerns for Archival Collections." *AB Bookman's Weekly* 88 (October 14, 1991): 1440-1444.

Lieberman's recommendations are based on those of the American Library Association's (ALA) Association for College and Research Libraries (ACRL), although he doesn't agree with all of the guidelines. Most notably, he asserts that withdrawn items should be canceled with a small mark, denoting where the withdrawn item was sent.

Menges, Gary L., ed. "ACRL Guidelines for the Security of Rare Book Manuscript and Other Special Collections." *College & Research Libraries News* 51 (March 1990): 240-244.

Recognizing the need for guidelines on the security of special collections, the Rare Books and Manuscript Section (RBMS) section of the ALA, drafted these principles. The guidelines cover every facet of collection security — from the security officer to the staff, the photocopiers, and legal responsibilities. The kinds of ink used in marking items and security equipment are also discussed.

— — — . "Security of Rare Books, Manuscripts, and Special Collections." *PNLA Quarterly* 53 (1989): 18.

Rare book thefts were increasing at an alarming rate in the 1980's. Menges cites specific cases, and refers to professional association guidelines (see above). He ends by adding his own guidelines that include increasing staff awareness and determining which items are the most valuable in the collection.

Newman, John. "Security in a Closed Environment." *Colorado Libraries* 11 (September 1985): 14-15.

Focusing on special collections and archival materials, Newman takes a look at providing security for materials in special situations. The author states that effective security practices and competent librarianship have much in common. A curator's first priority should be the safety of the materials, and the second is the patron's use of these guarded materials. Newman admits that special collection librarians are known for their tendency to arrange their materials in many different ways. In some respects, this is not only a service issue, but also a security issue. Special collections are not meant to be browsed. Instead, the special collection librarian or curator needs to talk with the patron to determine what the needs are, then fetch the materials for the researcher. Newman agrees that institutions should have policies that cover the security of special collections.

Overman, Linda. "Managing the Archival Environment: Environmental and Security Issues." *Mississippi Libraries* 59 (Summer 1995): 38-40.

Damage to library collections comes in several different forms. Environmental hazards, such as insects, humidity, pollutants, water, and human hazards are the two primary concerns for the archivist. Overman gives a good overview of environmental factors that need to be considered when keeping a special collection safe. She also briefly looks at theft of collections. If you want solid, basic information on environmental factors affecting archival materials, this article will fill your need.

"Safeguarding the Prints and Photographs Collections: Reading Room Will Launch Pilot Project." *Library of Congress Information Bulletin* 53 (January 10, 1994): 3-4.

For anyone who has been to the Library of Congress, one of the most impressive memories is not only the vast nature of the collection and the buildings, but the security measures that are in place. This article relates to the pilot project that the Prints and Photographs Division launched to limit the number of people in the reading room. A limit of eight walk-in patrons and three patrons with appointments has been mandated. Other special collection reading rooms have taken similar steps. This new policy should help alleviate the strain on the reference staff's ability to provide proper supervision of the reading rooms. With as many as thirty patrons at one time in one of these rooms, reference personnel found that it was becoming increasingly difficult to provide the assistance that the patrons needed.

Samuel, Evelyn. "Protection of Library and Archival Materials: A Case Study." *Library & Archival Security Newsletter* 2 (October 1979): 1-6.
This article takes an interesting approach to securing library collections — that is, allowing materials to be photocopied. The author looks at New York University's Institute of Fine Arts' library, where there are no closed-circuit televisions, no uniformed guards, and no electronic sensing devices. Instead, a friendly middle-aged man examines bags and briefcases and a photocopy machine has been installed. In addition to traditional photocopying, some materials are also photographed and made into slides.

"Security Guidelines of Rare Books, Manuscripts and Other Special Collections." *PNLA Quarterly* 53 (Winter 1989): 19.
These guidelines were written by the Rare Books and Manuscript Section of ACRL and are the recommended steps to follow in setting up an adequate security program. The first priority is that a senior staff member should be appointed the library security officer. Next, a policy should be written that includes procedures on dealing with theft. The special collection's physical attributes are detailed. Pointers, such as how to balance the responsibility of making materials available to patrons while ensuring their safety, are given.

Shockowitz, Tonya. "Security Issues for Archives, Rare Books, and Special Collections: A Bibliographic Essay." *Current Studies in Librarianship* 19 (Spring/Fall 1995): 4-12.
Security issues surrounding special collections and rare books have been concerns for librarians for many years. Nineteen articles covering issues and trends in security methods and guidelines are summarized.

Strassberg, Richard. "The Final Barrier: Security Considerations in Restricted Access Reading Rooms." *The Reference Librarian* 56 (1997): 95-105.

This article gives excellent, common-sense advice on preventing theft of materials from a reading room.

Traister, Daniel. "Seduction and Betrayal: An Insider's View of Insider Theft of Rare Materials." *Wilson Library Bulletin* 69 (September 1994): 30-33.

Insider theft is a real problem in some rare book rooms. This article details an example of inside theft and gives ideas for preventing theft.

Trinkaus-Randall, Gregor. "Library and Archival Security Policies and Procedures to Protect Holdings from Theft and Damage." *Journal of Library Administration* 25 (1998): 91-112.

This article is very similar in philosophy to his 1989 article that follows. Access versus security and preservation concerns are issues that are still present. The section on environmental concerns is interesting and contains some very good advice.

———. "Preserving Special Collections through Internal Security." *College & Research Libraries* 50 (July 1989): 448-454.

There is a fine line between keeping special collections secure yet still having them available to researchers. By carefully designing reading rooms and writing policies and procedures that cover theft and security of special collections, libraries can satisfy all people. Security programs have to keep in mind the staff, the patrons, and the collections. One of the keys to a program's success is the involvement of staff in the planning and design of the program. When designing the reading room, keep outerwear, umbrellas, book bags, briefcases, etc., in a separate area and only allow paper, personal computers, and writing instruments in the room. Consider requesting that patrons make appointments to use the archival materials. Also consider making copies for patrons rather than offering self-service.

Walsh, Jim. *Rare and Valuable Government Documents: A Resource Packet on Identification, Preservation, and Security Issues for Government Documents Collections.* Chicago: American Library Association, 1992. 125pp.

This publication is a joint effort of several ALA groups: the Government Documents Round Table, the Rare Books and Manuscripts Section, and the Geography Round Table. It is written in seven parts, each detailing a specific area. Part one is a bibliography; part two contains policies on preservation; part three has a summary of conference papers on identifying rare documents; part four consists of articles on conservation and preservation; part five discusses security issues; part six is a checklist of information needed for disaster planning; and part seven lists organizations that are sources of information in the preservation field.

Wurzburger, M. "Current Security Practices in College and University Special Collections." *Rare Books and Manuscripts Librarianship* 3 (1988): 43-57.

Sixty academic libraries completed a survey on security practices, and after analyzing the results, Wurzburger concluded that in the majority of libraries, access to special collections is controlled, bookplates are more favorable than electronic tagging, and the number of items a patron can use at one time is limited. Some libraries have installed buzzers on their doors and ask patrons to leave the section if the librarian has to step out of the room. Proper screening of potential employees is also important, and some libraries bond their special collection staffs.

Wyly, M. "Special Collections Security: Problems, Trends and Consciousness." *Library Trends* 36 (1987): 241-256.

Library security methods of 1987 were not much different than they were in the late 1960s. Wyly stresses the importance of re-evaluating these methods. Thieves are becoming more savvy, yet security methods have remained stagnant. He recommends hiring security staff and writing policies and procedures that point to more pro-active security measures.

Preservation Issues

American Association of Law Libraries, Special Committee on Preservation Needs of Law Libraries. "Preservation Treatment Options for Law Libraries." *Law Library Journal* 84 (Spring 1992): 265.

This article covers preservation treatments available for law library materials, but the information is appropriate to all types of library materials. Even though there are measures that can be taken to treat damaged items, the primary goals of disaster preparedness should be to respond quickly and provide speedy treatment of items if needed.

Barber, Giles. "Noah's Ark, or Thoughts Before and After the Flood." *Archives* 16 (1983): 151-161.

Suggestions for cleaning and drying water-damaged books are given. Mold is a critical problem and can set in quickly. Barber pays close attention to preventing mold from growing.

Bond, Randall, Mary DeCarlo, Elizabeth Henes, and Eileen Snyder. "Preservation Study at the Syracuse University Libraries." *College & Research Libraries* 48 (March 1987): 132-146.

The authors look at Syracuse University's survey of preservation problems at the university library. Randomly sampling 2,548 books, it was found that more than 25% were in need of repair and 20% were mutilated. One-half of the sampled books were "environmentally" damaged.

Child, Margaret. "Preservation Issues for Collection Development Staff." *Wilson Library Bulletin* 67 (November 1992): 20-22.

A library's mission should dictate which part of the collection should receive special preservation treatment. Some libraries have a commitment to collect certain materials, and it is these materials that should receive top priority.

Chamberlain, William R. "Fungus in the Library." *Library & Archival Security* 4 (1982): 35-38.

In 1978 the Virginia State Library suffered a severe fungal outbreak that lasted for three years. Don't worry that this article is sixteen years old; the same thing can happen again. Chamberlain details the conditions in the library during the outbreak and continues to follow the reporting through, to the identification of the fungus and different methods of control.

Ezennia, Steve E. "Flood, Earthquake, Libraries, and Library Materials." *Library & Archival Security* 13 (1995): 21-27.

Written by an acquisitions librarian from Anamdi Azikiwe University Library in Nigeria, this article gives an international perspective on an equally problematic issue for the United States. Some of the more useful advice is if materials get wet, act quickly to dry them and take precautionary methods to keep fungus from growing. In addition, make certain the library building has been constructed in accordance with national safety codes.

Fox, Lisa L. "A Two-Year Perspective on Library Preservation: An Annotated Bibliography." *Library Resources and Technical Services* 30 (July-September 1986): 290-318.

This annotated bibliography was compiled solely to raise the consciousness about librarians taking better care of their collections. There are several citations included in Fox's bibliography that aren't included here.

Harris, C. "The Preservation Considerations in Electronic Security Systems." *Library & Archival Security* 11 (1991): 17-22.

Electronic tags are harmful to the materials to which they are adhered. Harris denounces the importance of electronic security systems and discourages the use of tags. She proposes that materials be evaluated to determine if they are so important to the collection as to warrant tags.

Hickin, Norma. *Bookworms: The Insect Pests of Books*. London: Sheppard Press, 1985. 176pp.

Bookworms operate in silence and over a period of time weaken and destroy books. Although the term "worm" is a misnomer, these larval insects cause headaches to both the preservationist and the human bookworm. The author has her PhD in entomology and has spent four decades studying insects. This book has a wealth of information on book-eating pests and even though the language is in layperson's terms, the scientific names of the bookworms are given in the index.

Lowry, Marcia Duncan. *Preservation and Conservation in the Small Library*. Chicago, IL: American Library Association, Library Administration and Management Association, 1989. 15pp.

This small pamphlet discusses cost-effective measures small libraries can take to preserve their collections. Lowry points out that it is more cost effective to preserve a collection than to replace it.

Lunde, Diane B. "Do You Know Where Your Books Are?" *Colorado Libraries* 23 (Spring 1997): 41-42.

What if your library's books were stolen? Are they easily identified? Do you have a security system? Lunde reports on the necessity of properly marking library books as a security measure. Marking collections should be done with care and preservation of the materials in mind. Marking ink should be non-bleeding, non-acidic, non-fading, and indelible. Red ink is not advised because it tends to bleed. Book-plates should be acid-free and adhered using acid-free glue.

Morrow, Carolyn Clark and Carole Dyal. *Conservation Treatment Procedures: A Manual of Step-by-Step Procedures for the Maintenance and Repair of Library Materials.* Littleton, CO: Libraries Unlimited, 1985. 225pp.

This book is exactly what the title portrays, a step-by-step manual. It is clearly written and easy to follow. It is a very good resource manual for libraries with their own repair units or preservation labs.

Ogden, Sherelyn. "Security from Loss: Water and Fire Damage, Biological Agents, Theft, and Vandalism." *Rare Books & Manuscripts Librarianship* 11 (1996): 43-47.

Disaster planning should take into account all hazards. Ogden takes a close look at the effects water, fire, biological agents, and other hazards have on a collection and gives some steps to take in the event one of these harms your collection.

Patkus, Beth. "Collections Security: The Preservation Perspective." *Journal of Library Administration* 25 (1998): 67-89.

Patkus takes a broad interpretation of collection security and covers its preservation aspects. Environmental control, disaster preparedness, fire protection, storage and handling, and controlling access to collections are all discussed. This article is part of an entire issue of *Journal of Library Administration* that is devoted solely to management of library security.

Scott, Marianne. "Mass Deacidification at the National Library of Canada." *Library & Archival Security* 8 (1988): 49-52.

The preservation of the printed word is a concern for librarians and archivists alike. Acid decay has caused and will continue to cause the demise of books. Deacidification is a conservation measure. While it cannot restore strength to weakened pages, it can make damaged books seem to come back to life. The author takes a close descriptive look at the Wei T'o System, created in 1974 by Richard D. Smith. After four years in the pilot stages, the system was finally completed in 1978, and three years later it was fully operational.

Senadeera, N.T.S.A. "Microfilming for the Safety of Library Materials." *Information Development* 7 (October 1991): 208-212.

Microfilming of library materials is not new, but isn't thought of too often as a preservation tool. This article discusses the use of microfilming for the preservation of deteriorating materials at the University of Peradeniya, Sri Lanka.

Stazicker, Elizabeth. "Climatic Control: A Hopeless Bewilderment?" *Journal of the Society of Archivists* 8 (1987): 171-173.
Climate control is very important when it comes to preserving paper and parchment. Central heating and air-conditioning play havoc with controlling humidity and temperature in a library. Other environmental agents, such as dust and pollutants, can also harm books.

Swartzburg, Susan G. *Preserving Library Materials: A Manual.* 2nd ed. Metuchen, NJ: Scarecrow Press, 1995. 282pp.
Swartzburg takes the reader from the history of book preservation through environmental factors and the conservation of other materials, such as videotapes and phonograph records. The American Institute for the Conservation of Historic and Artistic Works code of ethics is included, as are an extensive glossary and a bibliography.

Underhill, K. and R. Butler. "T'was the Day after Christmas. . ." *Conservation Administration News* 46 (July 1991): 12-14.
When a 2-inch water main crossing the ceiling over a row of library stacks burst, the Cline Library at the University of Northern Arizona found itself flooded. Nearly 15,000 volumes were removed, and remarkably, only two were total losses.

4. COMPUTER AND TECHNOLOGY SECURITY

Computers are ever present in all libraries, and to make security issues confusing, most libraries not only have stand-alone personal computers, they also have computer networks and networks of networks. In addition, there are public workstations that hundreds of different people can use each day and there are data lines that allow patrons to bring in their own computers, plug into a jack, and instantly get connected to the library's network.

The Internet

Let's first look at the Internet. The Internet was born in the late 1960s when the United States Department of Defense connected computers in Colorado, Utah, and California together via phone lines. By the 1970s the military was using the network, and finally in the 1980s the National Science Foundation set up a high-capacity data backbone network (NSFnet), which soon became the infrastructure of the Internet. The Internet is huge, and because of its vast size, there is no way one person or one organization could be responsible for it. With the development of the transmission control protocol/Internet protocol standard (TCP/IP), communication among networks has become easy. TCP/IP is fast and simple but security is not a priority.

The Internet is used for E-mail, remote log-in, and file transfer. Remote log-in is possible with Telnet because Telnet allows access to systems and the world. Transferring documents electronically generally calls for a file transfer protocol (FTP). Other Internet tools have made their presences known during the past few years. GOPHER, USENET, and the World Wide Web are all systems that allow textual materials to be accessed through the Internet. The web, as everyone knows, provides not only textual information but also graphics. The web is based on a hypertext transfer protocol (HTTP) that runs on top of an extension of TCP/IP.

As can be seen, the Internet is vast and holds the key to fast, seamless access of materials by anyone from anyplace. The downside is that the Internet is not run by one person or one organization. It has been said that the Internet is only as strong as its weakest link. Maintenance of the Internet is a mind-boggling task, and maintenance of a library's network can be equally time consuming and challenging. Libraries depend on a freely functioning network. For that reason, and because libraries make significant investments in computer technology, they need to provide protection of their hardware and software.

UNIX environments are based on open systems and security issues are abundant. Even though the Internet as we know it today wouldn't exist without the UNIX operating system, there are so many well-known ways to "crack" the system that security is a real problem. Crackers can "finger" a system and receive a list of all users presently logged on; from there, a particular individual can be "fingered," and the amount and kind of information that can be obtained is limitless (Forcht and Fore, 1995). These are only a couple ways a UNIX system can be breached. There are others, and with each, the data that organizations think is safely tucked away can actually be easily accessed.

Fire walls, built between the Internet and the internal network, are one way to provide protection. A fire wall is a collection of networking components that are placed between an open network and a private network. If there is no fire wall, hackers can directly connect to the private network through any open network, such as the Internet (Chapman and Zwiecky, 1995).

Another Internet security protocol is one developed by Netscape Communications Corporation called the Secure Socket Layer (SSL). SSL offers security for Internet client-server applications with encryption and authentication done at the level of the socket library calls (Kou, 1997).

Java is another security device consisting of a programming language that runs on different types of computers. It is purported to be an ideal language for Internet programming; however, it has been speculated that there are potential problems (Sherman, 1997). Nonetheless, Java has been proven to offer security at various levels: package, abstract layer, application programming interface (API), application wide object, and low level.

Public Workstations

Public workstations offer different types of security problems because public workstations provide access to the Internet, and because most have hard drives and disk drives, computers are vulnerable. Some public workstations use a setup utility program that is activated by pressing a function key during the booting process. While some computers require that the system be booted from a disk, others can be set up to allow the system to boot from the hard drive. This latter setup eliminates the necessity of using the disk drive (Biever, 1997). However, this option doesn't protect the floppy drives from being breached. Some computer lab managers disable the floppy drives or cover the openings to disallow their use.

Keyboards have also been the causes of some security problems. Most notably, this has been by the use of the F1 or F2 key to launch the setup utility, the alt key to prevent a warm boot of the system, and the F5 or F8 key to break the boot sequence and allow an optional execution of each boot command (Brakel, 1997). By disabling these keys, some added security can be gained.

Depending on the software, there are several types of security files that can be used to control the environment. Some of these are Tweak UI, WinU, and Ikiosh (Marmion, 1997). A new problem that is beginning to surface is the convenience of spare jacks that are available for patrons to use in case they bring their own laptops. The main drawback with open jacks is they are invitations to hackers.

Hackers and Crackers

There are dozens of methods that can be used to provide security for library networks and workstations. As with any computer application, these methods change as fast as computer software changes. There are expensive solutions as well as inexpensive ones. Some are quick, Band-Aid solutions, while others are labor intensive. Nonetheless, there is seldom a system that is completely free from a possible breach, so caution must be practiced. Hackers, crackers, spammers, infiltrators — these are all different words for the same thing: someone who has breached and/or compromised a computer system. There probably isn't a library in existence that hasn't had its computer system broken into. Sometimes these are simple, mindless breaches, such as getting into the hard drive and installing games, pornographic software, and other similar, mischievous antics. Other breaches are very serious and consist of stealing data or installing a virus that shuts down the system and wipes out the data and the hard drive. Occasionally, hackers will come and go silently and unnoticed, but other times they call attention to themselves and leave messages alerting network managers that they've been there.

Perhaps one of the more frustrating issues when dealing with hackers is identifying the intruders. Hackers generally aren't anywhere near the systems they have infiltrated. They could be down the street or thousands of miles away. In fact, networks are so interwoven that it's possible to breach several systems in different states at once.

What steps should be taken to catch a hacker? First, you need to decide if it's necessary to catch/identify the hacker because this task can be tedious and time consuming. However, there are situations where the hackers have been threatening or have stolen data, and the people responsible for those crimes need to be identified and prosecuted. The most efficient method to use to catch a hacker is to involve the local police and, if appropriate, federal authorities (Rosachi, 1997).

In all the literature, the same advice is given: document, document, document, and save files on a daily basis. Some other advice includes:

- keep an eye out for abnormal usage and look for users who are logged on to the system for long periods of time,
- log everything, and note the time of the logs,
- make contact with authorities who have knowledge of computer crime and can give you advice on what information to collect and how to collect it,
- know the software you are using,
- try to break into your own system (German, 1997)

There is an over-abundance of literature about computer security. Although computer technology is a fast-changing field, the articles that are cited below are broad enough to be of interest regardless of the changes in software and/or hardware.

Citations

Computer Technology Security

Aldridge, Alicia, Michele White, and Karen A. Forcht. "Security Considerations of Doing Business Via the Internet: Cautions to be Considered." *Internet Research* 7 (1997): 9-15.

The World Wide Web has opened up a whole realm of possibilities for doing research and conducting business. This article takes a long look at some of the security problems associated with doing business using the web.

Anderson, Laura Challman. *Rights Management and Security in the Electronic Library.* Yorktown Heights, NY: IBM Research Division, 1995. 8pp.

This pamphlet primarily discusses the management of intellectual property and confidentiality of usage data, but some general security features are also given. Because more and more resources are being digitalized, this is an emerging and important security issue that libraries are only now beginning to face. This pamphlet can also be found in article format in *Bulletin of the American Society for Information Science* 22 (October-November 1995): 21-23.

Balas, Janet. "Protecting the Network." *Computers in Libraries* 17 (November/December 1997): 34-38.

Libraries and computers go hand in hand, and Balas takes an informative look at maintaining a library network system and offers tips on how to keep it secure. Some of the resources she discusses include Netsurfer Focus, Computer Emergency Response Team (CERT) Coordination Center, and Java Security Frequently Asked Questions (FAQ).

"Baltimore Technologies Releases Secure Messaging Toolkit; Developers Toolkit for Fast, Easy Implementation of Security into any Messaging Application." *Business Wire* (January 11, 1998). Wire service.

One of the newest technologies in the computer security field is a messaging toolkit built on top of Baltimore Technologies' Crypto System Toolkit. The secure messaging toolkit (SMT) software ensures that mail is confidential and not altered in transit.

Bar-Ilan, Judit. "Security Issues on the Internet." *The Electric Library* 14 (February 1996): 37-42.

No one can refute that the Internet is a very large mass of networks. With the advent of TCPs/IPs, electronic communication is easy. However, as Bar-Ilan admits, the Internet is not security conscientious. Using that premise, she explains how some institutions guard themselves against intruders. Some of these precautions include using smart cards and employing cryptography.

The bulk of the article is on cryptosystems, and the information given is well documented and thoroughly explained.

Benson, Allen C. "Building a Secure Library System." *Computers in Libraries* 18 (March 1998): 24-26, 28-29.

Using a real-life encounter with a hacker, Benson relates his experiences at keeping his library's system secure and hacker proof. First, you need to determine what is at risk and then take steps to reduce those risks. Next, a disaster plan and a security policy should be written. Even though all of these are time consuming, they are necessary housekeeping tasks. Benson concludes with the statement that the key is to protect the library's computer system without hindering the ability to access information.

Biemiller, Laurence. "U.S. Plans New Effort on Computer Security." *Chronicle of Higher Education* 44 (March 27, 1998): A33.

The United States Department of Justice has begun to organize a $64 million effort to make computer networks less vulnerable to break-ins. The plan will establish a National Infrastructure Protection Center that will serve as a clearinghouse for information about computer break-ins.

Biever, Erik. "Securing Public Workstations by Maintaining Software Centrally." *Library Hi Tech* 15 (1997): 27-29.

This article focuses on the University of Minnesota-Twin Cities libraries. With 150 Windows-based personal computer (PC) workstations available for public use, the libraries have a challenging task to maintaining their system's security. The libraries don't want users to boot from a diskette, so that option is disabled. In addition, certain features of Netscape Navigator are blocked. Biever details the libraries' remote software maintenance schedule and includes the Uniform Resource Locator (URL) for different workstation software, administration tools, and server software.

Brakel, Garvin. "Public Workstation Security." *Library Hi Tech* 15 (1997): 24-26.

The Spokane (Washington) Public Library serves a community of 186,000 and has 100 public workstations that run Windows 95 and Netscape Navigator. Brakel concentrates on what can be done to secure the operating system and gives pointers on protecting the hardware. Most computer security articles discuss system security, but the advantage of this article over others is that it also gives ideas on protecting the hardware. Some of these ideas are to secure the mouse by wiring the cable to the connection and to cover the floppy drive with aluminum flashing. The tips he gives are cost effective and easy enough for any computer lab manager to initiate.

Breeding, Marshall. "Designing Secure Library Networks." *Library Hi Tech* 15 (1997): 11-20.

There are several options that libraries can use to provide protection for their networks. Of course, high security does not come cheaply, but recovering from a breach in security is also expensive. Breeding thoroughly examines the characteristics of library computer networks and the vulnerability of systems. He includes several diagrams that clearly show the relationships between a network and a router.

Bridgeman, C. "Foolproof Solutions for the Foolhardy." *Disaster Recovery Journal* 7 (April/May 1994): 77.

Computer data is just as vulnerable to loss as print materials. Bridgeman discusses some of the methods by which computer data can be lost, whether it is through a natural disaster or by hacking.

Camp, Jean and Doug Tygor. *Providing Auditing while Protecting Privacy: the Special Case of Library Information Systems.* Pittsburgh, PA: School of Computer Science, Carnegie Mellon University, 1993. 27pp.

Although this publication really is a research paper, it gives pertinent information on the security of microdata and library records in general. Carnegie Mellon University's library information system, LISII, was used to illustrate the security issues involved. Network security, microdata security, and legal models of privacy are covered in part one. Part two examines library information systems, and part three considers system categories and comparisons.

Chapman, D. Brent and Elizabeth D. Zwicky. *Building Internet Firewalls.* Sebastopol, CA: O'Reilly and Associates, 1995. 554pp.

Network security, building fire walls, and keeping your site secure are all covered. In other words, this is a practical handbook on how to build your own Internet security. The majority of the book is about tactics or how-to ideas, but there is a section on writing a security policy that goes beyond a simple how-to guide. Instead, it is convincing and detailed. Network managers and system administrators should be aware of the protocols and security strategies given in this book.

Cheswick, William R. and Steven M. Bellovin. *Firewalls and Internet Security.* Reading, MA: Addison-Wesley, 1994. 306pp.

This book is written expressly for the network administrator with a UNIX operating system. The focus is on TCPs/IPs and on the Internet. Every detail associated with computer security is covered beginning with particular security issues associated with TCPs/IPs and going into fire walls, gateways, and hacker's tools. The book ends with information on the legal implications of computer security. An interesting feature is Appendix C, recommendations to vendors. In this section, the authors have listed different recommendations to designers and vendors of networking equipment. Also given is information on free packages that can be downloaded from the Internet and used to secure your own network.

Cole, Timothy W. "Mosaic on Public Access PC's: Letting the World Wide Web into the Library." *Computers in Libraries* 15 (January 1995): 44-50.

The majority of this article is about the full connection between OPACs and the Internet at the University of Illinois' engineering library's information center. But one part is dedicated to the steps the library took to reduce public access PC software security risks. These four easy steps are: 1) AUTOEXEC.BAT automatically launches the main public access menu program; 2) the library has set the read-only attribute for most files; 3) MOSAIC is launched from its own Windows menu program; and 4) the library starts Windows with a pair of DOS batch files that call each other.

— — —. "Using Bluestem for Web User Authentication and Access Control of Library Resources." *Library Hi Tech* 15 (1997): 58-71.

Bluestem is a web authentication and access control system the University of Illinois recently developed. Cole explains how the program works to control end-user access to bibliographic resources.

Covington, Michael A. "Design and Implementation of a Campus Computer Ethics Policy." *Internet Research* 5 (1995): 31-41.

Covington presents the University of Georgia's computer ethics policy and goes through the process of developing the policy. One issue that was of importance is that computer ethics change from year to year; therefore, the policy has to be rewritten to accommodate the changes. Once written, the policy is then distributed to the campus community. Ads in newspapers and posters with the policy printed on them were also used. Libraries or universities in the process of writing policies would be wise to read this article and follow some of the suggestions.

Curry, David A. *UNIX System Security: A Guide for Users and System Administrators.* Reading, MA: Addison-Wesley, 1992. 279pp.

Just as the subtitle states, this is a guide for both users and system administrators. In the preface, Curry mentions that UNIX systems were not originally designed with security in mind. During the past twenty years, more businesses and universities have started to run UNIX systems for their confidential and sensitive programs. With the advances in UNIX programs and the wide usage of the systems, security problems have become more difficult to control. Curry reviews UNIX systems and talks about encryption software and how to respond to system attacks. He ends the book with Purdue (Indiana) University's computer network policy on access and usage.

"Data Security and Privacy in the Age of Automated Library Systems." *Online Libraries and Microcomputers* 6 (February 1, 1998). Electronic publication.

Personal information found in library databases has become a security issue. As computers become more sophisticated, it is easier for outsiders to access this confidential information. This article takes a thorough look at this concern and offers some practical advice to follow to protect sensitive data.

Delaney, Tom. "Necessity is the Mother of Virtuality." *Colorado Libraries.* 24 (Fall 1998): 13-15.

As head of Interlibrary Loan, Delaney knows first hand what obstacles and issues arise when a disaster hits. Although the physical space was untouched, all power and telecommunications had been knocked out when a natural disaster hit Colorado State University in the summer of 1997. Delaney covers all aspects of interlibrary loan operations including implementing new programs that enhance the access to materials.

Delfino, Erik. "Developing Your Security Savvy." *Online* 20 (July/August 1996): 78-79.

Starting with the premise "You can't trust anyone," the author reiterates the importance of keeping PCs and information secure. Even though computer viruses get most of the publicity, they are only one of the threats. There are several other security aspects: passwords, user identifications, and encrypted data.

Doddrell, Gregory R. "Information Security and the Internet." *Internet Research* 6 (1996): 5-9.
   Security issues in libraries aren't only about paper materials. Most libraries have their holdings stored on computer disks or tapes and/or they use computers to aid in cataloging and acquisitions. What is thought to be easy access to the collection by patrons is exactly that — easy access by anyone. Doddrell identifies the risks, suggests solutions, and illustrates what happens when a network is not adequately protected.

Drewes, Jeanne. "Computers: Planning for Disaster." *Law Library Journal* 81 (Winter 1989): 103-116.
   Drewes contends that a good disaster plan divides the workload logically and that to protect computers in the event of a disaster, they need to be written into the disaster plan. This article explains the importance of including computer security in the disaster plan, ways to guard loss, and how to provide protection. Some of the suggestions Drewes gives are back-up data and store the back-up tapes or disks off-site; remove harmful elements such as dust, water, heat, and humidity from the computer environment; use a disk-drive cover to protect the hardware; install covers on printers; and turn off computers at night if an automatic shutdown system isn't installed.

Erlanger, Leon. "Disarming the Net." *PC Magazine* 16 (June 10, 1997): NE1-5.
   Making technology available to employees within and outside the confines of the library is something that network managers are well versed in; however, keeping these connections "safe" is an entirely different matter. Systems generally are rather easy to infiltrate, thereby forcing organizations to take measures to ensure the security of their computers and network systems. This article gives a guide to follow when securing the Internet. First, a security policy should be written that details which employees have access to which services and what the consequences are for breaches of the system. Second, a barrier between internal and external networks and a filter of incoming and outgoing data is necessary. These are called fire walls. Third, authentication of actual users is needed; fourth, an encryption algorithm should be used in order to prevent E-mail or Internet transactions from being intercepted;

and fifth, virtual private networks (VPN) help create a "tunnel" between two sites. In addition to being well written and thorough, this article offers the reader a host of Internet security products that can provide the security needed.

Fites, Philip E. *Information Systems Security: A Practitioner's Reference.* New York: Van Nostrand Reinhold, 1993. 471pp.

This guide covers a broad range of security topics and is written for the network manager/analyst. It also describes the Computer Security Act that was written in 1987. This act requires that corporations adopt general security policies. Three factors must be covered in the policy: sensitive systems and data need to be identified; plans for ensuring the security and control of such systems should be created; and personal training programs must be developed. This manual also covers cryptography, telecommunication security, legal and regulatory issues, policy development, and information ethics.

Forcht, Karen A. and Richard E. Fore. "Security Issues and Concerns with the Internet." *Internet Research* 5 (1995): 23-31.

In simplistic terms, the Internet is a network of networks. There are more than 30,000 networks with 3 million host computers and thirty-five million users (as of 1995). Born in the late 1960s, the Internet continues to grow and along with this growth have come problems such as security and keeping data safe. Because the Internet is a decentralized system, it is vulnerable to electronic attacks. Once an intruder gets in, access to all parts is easily accomplished. CERT was formed using federal money to watch over the Internet and to study ways hackers gain access. Most servers on the Internet are based on systems such as UNIX. In a UNIX environment, there are five well-known ways to crack the system. To help provide security for the Internet, fire walls are built and sometimes router filters are also used.

Fore, Julie A. "Things That Go Bump In the Virtual Night." *Library Hi Tech* 15 (1997): 84-91.

All one needs to do to get a library's system administrator upset is to talk about a security breach in a server. Fore's article is an informative piece on server security that includes short side articles by Don Simpson, president of the Center for Research Libraries and Marshall Breeding, library technology analyst at Vanderbilt University in Nashville, Tennessee. She gives advice on some very practical issues. These include looking into what kind of condition the hardware is in. How old is it? Do multiple people use the system? Where is the server housed? How complex is the operating system?

Forester, Tom and Perry Morrison. *Computer Ethics: Cautionary Tales and Ethical Dilemmas in Computing.* Cambridge, MA: MIT Press, 1990. 193pp.

Computers have made a myriad of information and literature sources readily available at one's fingertips. Along with this has come the need for computer ethics. Chapter six, "The Invasion of Privacy," studies legislation, surveillance, and database disasters. It is common that computers are breached and while some breaches are meant to be harmful, others are simply an invasion of privacy. Regardless what occurs on your system, if the system has been compromised measures should be taken to warrant that the breaches won't occur again.

Fouty, Kathleen G. "Online Patron Records and Privacy: Service vs. Security." *Journal of Academic Librarianship* 19 (November 1993): 289-293.

Online circulation systems have opened up a new area of security concerns for librarians. Considerable information is stored in a patron's record, such as social security number, address, and phone number. Fouty's article addresses these concerns and gives several very good suggestions on limiting the data collected, ensuring compliance with policies, and creating and modifying patron records.

Fredman, David H. and Charles C. Mann. "Cracker." *U.S. News and World Report 122* (June 2, 1997): 56.

This article is one that you won't be able to put down. The authors relate tales of crackers, or electronic burglars, who break into computers. They look at crackers with names like "#hack," "Phantom Dialer," "Grob," and "Crack." Not only is this article entertaining, it is also an eye-opener. Could this really happen to your system?

Furnell, Steven M. and Matthew J. Warren. "Computer Abuse: Vandalizing the Information Society." *Internet Research* 7 (1997): 61-66.

Computers have made work easier, but they have also brought about serious security concerns. Furnell and Warren examine some of these issues in this insightful article.

Garfinkle, Simson. *PGP: Pretty Good Privacy.* Sebastopol, CA: O'Reilly and Associates, 1994. 430pp.

What program can work on nearly every platform, uses a public key cryptography, and protects files and E-mail? PGP, developed by Phil Zimmermann, is a powerful tool, and everything anyone has ever wanted to know about it can be found in this book.

——— and Gene Spafford. *Practical UNIX Security* 2nd ed. Sebastopol, CA: O'Reilly and Associates, 1996. 800pp.

The first edition of this book was seen as being on the front line of UNIX security issues, but this second edition is completely revised and even more informative. Several platforms are covered, and new security tools are given.

Gaudin, Sharon and Sharon Machlis. "ActiveX Gets Security Boost." *Computerworld* 31 (June 16, 1997): 12.

Computer security is vital to any well-functioning organization. Microsoft has made its Authenticode 2.0 software available from its web site. Authenticode allows an ActiveX control to be digitally signed, thus allowing web users to decide if they trust the site's author before downloading the code to their machines.

Girard, Kim. "Laptop Thieves Beware." *Computerworld* 32 (December 29, 1997): 14.

Notebook computers are a computer thief's dream. They are small, light, and can be unplugged and concealed within seconds. This article is a product announcement for a new breed of security devices on the market to help catch laptop thieves. Two of the leading anti-theft products are Absolute Software's CompuTrace and Computer Sentry Software Inc.'s CyberAngel. Both operate on a monitoring system that checks either the password or the phone number being used. If either of these is incorrect, the computer alerts the authorized user via fax, pager, or E-mail.

Goldberg, Beverly. "Microchip Thefts Plague Southern California Libraries." *American Libraries* 27 (August 1996): 13-14.

Even though this article is only one full column in length, it is an excellent example of the vulnerability of library computers.

Icove, David, Karl Seger, and William Von Storch. *Computer Crime: A Crime Fighters Handbook.* Sebastopol, CA: O'Reilly and Associates, 1995. 464pp.

Computers and networks are attractive prey to hackers. Computer crimes can range from simple pranks and rearranging data to full-fledged financial crimes. This book focuses on computer crimes and serves as a step-by-step manual on what to do when a computer breach of security is suspected. A host of information is given about laws, criminal profiles, and how to prosecute computer crimes. One of the most worthwhile sections of this book is a compendium of federal and state statutes.

Ives, David J. "Security Management Strategies for Protecting Your Library's Network." *Computers in Libraries* 16 (February 1996): 36-39.

End users pose the greatest threat to a library's LAN security. This threat can be either deliberate or accidental. If deliberate, it can be attributed to: 1) boredom; 2) excitement of a challenge; 3) greed; 4) anger or dissatisfaction with the library; or 5) anger or frustration with everyone.

— — — . "The Four-Tiered Approach to Computer Network Security Management." *Computers in Libraries* 16 (February 1996): 39-40.

Not all security strategies for computer systems need be expensive to implement. Ives reports on a four-tiered approach that is low cost, not time consuming and protects computers, peripherals, and networks. The four areas involved are the hardware, the system, the network, and the user interface. To ensure that microcomputer central processing units (CPU) are protected, all network wiring closets should be kept locked; the CPU case should be integrally locked with its OEM-provided lock; and the CPU, monitor, and printer of each workstation should be cable-locked together. There are several programs and steps that can be taken to protect the network. Some of these include employing a replacement log-in program to prevent access to the F:\LOGIN directory; requiring that patron/public user log in names be account and station-restricted to only one concurrent log in and to only one specific computer; and enabling the network "Intruder Lockout" option and setting them for no more than three attempts.

— — — . "What a Security Program is Not." *Computers in Libraries* 16 (February 1996): 41.

There are four main things that a computer security program should not be: negotiable, secure by consensus, able to be compromised, and decentralized. Ives' short article briefly describes each.

Kou, Weidong. *Networking Security and Standards*. Boston, MA: Kluwer, 1997. 207pp.

This book responds to the need in the computer security marketplace for a simple, easy-to-understand, explanation of Internet security issues. The basic principles of Internet and computer security standards are explained.

Koulouthros, Yvonne and Melissa J. Perenson. "Virus Hunt: Part Two." *PC Magazine* 17 (February 10, 1998): 36.

Even though this article was out of date before it hit the stands, it still gives worthwhile advice on the varieties of virus kits that are available for Windows programs. Phone numbers of the program developers accompany the text, so you can get immediate advice about the software or information about software for Windows 98.

Lavagno, Merri Beth. "The ICAAP Project, Part One: A Continuum of Security Needs for the CIC Virtual Electronic Library." *Library Hi Tech* 15 (1997): 72-76.

The Committee on Institutional Cooperation (CIC) is an academic consortium of twelve major teaching and research universities that started the Virtual Electronic Library. Along with this electronic library, they created a security list that outlines the security and authentication issues that must be addressed. This article describes these concerns.

Machlis, Sharon. "Employee Participation Key to Successful Security." *Computerworld* 31 (July 28, 1997): 45.

Users have to be involved in developing computer security policies and programs. Systems analysts should meet and talk with key users and managers to identify which critical data and systems to protect. When drafting a plan, know what information is vital to the company. Who creates it and who needs access to it.

— — — . "Hackers Warn: Beware of NT Security Holes." *Computerworld* 31 (July 21, 1997): 49.

Windows NT hasn't been out long, but there already is widespread concern over hackers. It's not that NT is less secure than other commercial operating systems; it's because it is relatively new and the hacking community sees it as interesting prey. One simple step to take to secure a system is administration should turn off all operating system functions they don't need.

—— —. "Wrestling with Web Privacy." *Computerworld* 31 (June 23, 1997): 47-48.

Privacy over the Internet has long been discussed both among computer managers and novice web surfers. This article announces the first technical meeting of the World Wide Web Consortium in June 1997. Called the P3, Platform for Privacy Preferences, the consortium's goal is to help users decide whether to put personal information into the web or not. There are several issues surrounding web privacy and one of the most prominent statements is that privacy should be protected by law.

"Making the Web Safe for Commerce." *Crain's Chicago Business* 20 (March 3, 1997): 13.

Many online commercial firms have found that the current security standards, including secure socket layer encryption, are not adequate. This article takes a look at FastParts, an online program that offers a web service trading floor on which purchasers and sellers can negotiate prices. It is anticipated that technology will be added as security issues arise.

Marmion, Dan. "A Commercial Software Approach to Workstation Security." *Library Hi Tech* 15 (1997): 21-23.

Western Michigan University is a fairly typical research university library with 100 public computers. It recognizes the fact that there is a fine line between allowing patrons access to electronic databases and still keeping the system secure. Marmion describes the solution Western Michigan University came up with to protect its public workstations.

Martin, Susan K. *The Professional Librarian's Reader in Library Automation and Technology.* White Plains, NY: Knowledge Industry Publications, 1980. 201pp.

This volume is a broad look at library technology. The last chapter is a reprint of Alice Bahr's book, *Theft and Library Security Systems.* By looking at the copyright date, you can tell that this isn't going to be too involved with computer security; however, this book is a good historical overview.

McClure, Stuart. "Internet Scanner Fills the Holes." *InfoWorld* 20 (January 26, 1998): 66C.

This article describes one of the newest protection products on the market for Windows NT. Internet Security Systems' Internet Scanner performs security audits and locates potential holes. It scans web servers, fire walls, and routers; however, it is a bit expensive.

McMurdo, George. "Pretty Good Encryption." *Journal of Information Science* 22 (1996): 133-146.
Computer communication and the wide availability and usage of the Internet have made good encryption methods very important. McMurdo's article not only gives an interesting history lesson on cryptography, but it also informs the reader of more recent developments in encryption software.

Miller, R. Bruce. "Libraries and Computers: Disaster Prevention and Recovery." *Information Technology and Libraries* 7 (December 1988): 349-358.
A lot has changed in the computer field since this article was written, but the premise remains true: library computer systems are vulnerable. Miller examines natural catastrophes, computer failure, viruses, back up procedures, building security, and hardware theft. Read the suggestions while keeping in mind new software. The planning section is very pertinent to all libraries, regardless of whether it is 1988 or 2000. First, the planning process must be organized, then perform a risk assessment, develop disaster prevention strategies, draft survival strategies and a recovery process, and document the procedural guidelines, including who does what.

Opplinger, Rolf. *Authentication Systems for Secure Networks.* Boston: Artech House, 1996. 186pp.
This is one of the more recent books on computer security that covers the Internet and other network environments. Included is a glossary, as well as a list of abbreviations and acronyms. Each of the nine chapters describes different authentication and key distribution systems. MIT, IBM, and DEC developments are three of the six described.

Pearlstein, Joanna. "Purity Offers WebSentinel Public Beta." *MacWeek* 11 (June 9, 1997): 21-22.
Because it doesn't seem as though the web is going away any time soon, this article is important because it illustrates some of the software that is being developed to offer more security for information on the web. While some software is very expensive, this one is quite reasonably priced and includes a graphical administration application for managing server access and WebSentinel will run on any network.

"Physical Security of Library Computer Equipment." *Online Libraries and Microcomputers* 6 (May 1, 1998). Electronic publication.

There are several steps that should be taken to assess the current physical security of library computer equipment and it is important to remember that different levels of security are required for different situations. It is beneficial to have a checklist on hand to consult when assessing the equipment. This checklist should cover environmental/fire/electrical concerns, software, and physical access to the equipment.

Riley, Gordon. "Managing Microcomputer Security: Policy and Practice Considerations for CD-ROM and Public Access Workstations." *Library & Archival Security* 11 (1992): 1-15.

CD-ROM workstations have been subject to viruses that spread through downloading from floppy disks. Some of these viruses are introduced accidentally; others are deliberate. Riley examines computer viruses and their impact on academic libraries. Noting that in 1988 there were 39 known viruses and only four years later, there were more than 166 different strains, Riley surmises that viruses have become a type of hobby with some people. He continues by giving a case study of the Michigan's Wayne State University Purdy/Kresge Library that had experienced two virus strains in one year.

Russell, Deborah and G.T. Gangemi Sr. *Computer Security Basics*. Sebastopol, CA: O'Reilly and Associates, 1991. 464pp.

Computer security isn't simple, but after reading this manual, encryption and access control should become clearer. Readable and well organized, this book is filled with authoritative information and advice.

Saftner, Donald and Bhanu Raghunathan. "Privacy in the Computer Age." *Journal of Information Ethics* 4 (Fall 1995): 43-51.

Computers have made it easier to obtain information, and they have also made it easier to obtain personal or private information. The authors report the results from a computer privacy survey taken of students at a medium-sized midwestern university. According to the results, 79% of the respondents were concerned with invasion of personal property. After reviewing the answers to the thirteen questions on the survey, the authors noted that all in all, the respondents expressed a high level of concern about the privacy of computerized data.

Sherman, Erik. "Java Security Issues Brewing; Many Believe that Safety Should be Part of Tool Itself." *MacWeek* 11 (August 11, 1997): 21-22.

Java can be seen as a chameleon in the computer security arena. In many respects, it appears to be the answer because as an interpreted language, it can run across platforms, but this is also its downfall because this leaves it wide open to reverse engineering. There are products being developed to address the source-code security issues of Java, and JavaSoft, a division of Sun Microsystems, is addressing these issues itself. This article is included because it shows the susceptibility of software to new problems. What once was thought to be the answer to many problems has opened up other issues that need to be confronted.

Smith, Lorre. "Interactive Multi-Media and Electronic Media in Academic Libraries: Policy Implications." *Reference Librarian* 38 (1992): 229-244.

Reference services no longer solely rely on books. Electronic resources play an important role in providing efficient reference service. However, along with these new tools comes the necessity for policies that address security of electronic resources. Computer security must be included in the overall disaster plan for the library.

Spanbauer, Scott. "Bugs and Fixes." *PC World* 15 (September 1997): 53.

This is a regular feature column that gives the latest information on bugging and debugging software. Because technology changes so quickly, anyone wanting information on the newest computer security should consult Spanbauer's column.

Stallings, William. *Network and Internetwork Security.* Englewood Cliffs, NJ: Prentice-Hall, 1995. 480pp.

Network and Internet work protocols, standards, and security features are covered. This text doesn't assume that the reader has a vast knowledge of security issues such as encryption standards. A wide variety of computer security standards are covered and thoroughly explained.

Starrett, Bob. "Hide and Seek Announces Non-Intrusive CD Copy Protection." *EMedia Professional* 10 (August 1997): 13-14.

CD and DVD media can now be easily protected with a new development from Hide and Seek Technologies. The copy protection is added to the structure of the disk during the manufacturing process and is non-intrusive and transparent to the end user. It can be controlled either by the installation software or by the optical media and doesn't require modifications to CD-ROM or DVD-ROM drive designs.

Steinauer, Dennis D. "Security of Personal Computer Systems: A Management Guide." *Information Reports and Bibliographies* 14 (1985): 18-25.

Don't let the date of this article fool you; it still contains pertinent information on how to safe-guard your computer. Covered are basic security concerns, such as physical accessibility and built-in security mechanisms, and risk management issues. Also included is a self-audit questionnaire that covers physical and environmental protection, control of media, system and data access controls, electrical power quality control, and theft protection.

"Student Finds NT Security Hole." *Computerworld* 31 (July 14, 1997): 8.

A Russian student found a hole in Windows NT that allows local users to get administrative privileges and access to other users' files. Although only inside users, and not hackers, can gain access, the hole still has security implications for the organization.

Summers, Rita C. *Secure Computing.* New York: McGraw-Hill, 1997. 688pp.

There is hardly a single business that doesn't, in some way, use computer technology. Libraries have come a long way during the past twenty years, and computer technology plays a large role in the typical library's daily activities. However, coupled with the advent of computer technology into the library world, there is the threat of a system breach with the potential of destroying patron files, literature databases, employee payroll information, the on-line catalog, fire alarms, automatic lights, and sprinkler systems. Summers covers all aspects of making one's computer secure. Starting with the job of security management and taking the reader through policies, operations security analysis of one's system, network security, database security, and designing and building secure systems, the author leaves no issue untouched. This is a detailed, thorough look at the daunting task of computer security. It's not for the layperson, but every network manager should be aware of this book.

Sylvia, Margaret. "Upgrading a CD-ROM Network for Multimedia Applications." *Computers in Libraries* 15 (June 1995): 72-74.

There probably isn't a single library that doesn't have some sort of multimedia computer application. CD-ROMs and access to the Internet are becoming standard offerings. However, along with these applications also comes the problem of warranting the safety of the network. The first rule of thumb is to give patrons only the minimum rights needed to run the software. Sylvia continues and gives explicit directions on editing the PROGMAN.INI file.

Tweney, Dylan. "Lock Your Desktop." *PC Computing* 6 (1993): 258, 260.

Even though this "hot tip" is not a substantive article, it is very informative, and with the prevalence of laptops and notebook computers among librarians as well as corporate executives, it is information worth noting. In a nutshell, if your Windows shell is Program Manager, edit PROGMAN.INI to restrict access to its features. In Notepad or another text-only editor, open PROGMAN.INI and add the line [restrictions] to the end of the file. Then just add lines for the restrictions you want. Tweney continues and gives a step-by-step procedure for adding security restrictions to your laptop computer.

"Web Sites Gain Security, Efficiency." *Byte* 22 (August 1997): 24.

A 1997 survey showed that businesses want to ensure the security of their computer systems. Fire walls were listed as the top products to be purchased. In 1996 a similar survey pointed to website development tools as the number one planned purchase items.

Willson, Jonathan. "Open Doors in Cyberspace." *Library Association Record* 97 (November 1995 supplement): 19-20.

Computer technology has vastly improved the inner workings of all businesses, but it isn't without its problems. Personal information floats all around cyberspace and is simply waiting for someone to grab it. Confidentiality is a word of the past. Cyberspace knows no boundaries and transactions in cyberspace can take place under an assumed name. Anonymity is imperative for a number of people, and there are some precautions that can be implemented. Anonymous remailers are programs that strip an E-mail message of identifying information and forwards the message to the addressee. Anonymous services also allow a reply to be sent without an identifier. Anonymous file transfer protocol (FTP) lets users log in anonymously and transfer files and data.

Wrobel, Leo. *Disaster Recovery Planning for Telecommunications.* Boston: Artech, 1990. 112pp.

Even though this book is rather outdated in terms of computer security, it still contains worthwhile advice to heed when looking into contingency planning. As is true with most disaster preparedness measures, the worst-case scenario should be planned for. However, when it comes to telecommunication disasters, two questions should be asked: 1) is a total loss of the data center really the worst-case scenario, and 2) if so, is this the worst thing that could happen? Wrobel gives some thought-provoking statements that all computer network managers need to be aware of.

Hackers

Delaney, Tom. "If You Think Your System Hasn't Been Compromised, Think Again." *Computers in Libraries* 16 (February 1996): 18-20.

University library computer systems are perfect hiding places for hackers while they access or reroute other systems. The experiences the author writes about could very easily happen to other libraries. Delaney gives an account of what occurred, how the library focused on solving the problem, and what questions should be asked to determine the level of security you need to maintain.

German, Greg. "To Catch a Hacker." *Library Hi Tech* 15 (1997): 96-98.

After experiencing a breach of security, the Ohio Library and Information Network closely inspected what occurred and what it learned from the experience. These lessons include keep an eye out for abnormal usage, maintain a log of the software your system uses, try to break into your own software, and find someone knowledgeable about computer crime to help you obtain the proof you need to prosecute an intruder.

Golden, Ed. "IBM Burglar Alarm Detects Hackers." *InfoWorld* 19 (July 28, 1997): 25.

Hackers pose threats to every system, and preventing hackers from being successful seems to be an on going struggle for network technicians. IBM now has an Internet burglar alarm that lets IBM security experts detect attacks on customers' networks. This alarm is the third part of the triangle of IBM's Internet emergency response system.

Hafner, Katie and John Markoff. *Cyberpunk: Outlaws and Hackers on the Computer Frontier.* New York: Simon and Schuster, 1995.
Find out firsthand how a hacker thinks and plans what he or she wants to do, and build an arsenal against hacker infiltration by reading this book. The book profiles three hackers and gives interesting histories and revelations of their favorite hacking targets.

Knightmare, The. *The Secrets of a Super Hacker.* Port Townsend, WA: Loompanic Unlimited, 1994. 205pp.
Divided into three parts — before the hacking, during the hacking, and after the hacking — this book is a how-to manual for would-be hackers, and an even more valuable source of information for network managers. Of notable interest to libraries is the author's knowledge of public access computers. These include those in malls and banks as well as those in libraries. The author, a self professed hacker, covers on-site hacking, hacking from home, electronic bulletin boards, and what to do once you are in a system. Also covered are state and federal computer crime laws and what organizations can do to keep their systems secure. A glossary of computer terminology is included.

Landreth, Bill. *Out of the Inner Circle.* New York: Microsoft Press, 1989. 240pp.
As a reformed hacker, Landreth now spends his time educating others about computer security. A lot has changed since Landreth first hacked a system, but some of the tips he gives are still valuable for some older systems.

LaRue, James. "Confessions of a Hacker: Fear and Panic in the Information Age." *Colorado Libraries* 23 (Spring 1997): 12-15.
LaRue's article is an interesting case history of the time a community service worker compromised his system. Thinking he and his staff were doing their civic duty by providing some training and community service work hours, the author came to a rude awakening when he discovered that the young worker had easily found his way into the library's system. Some suggestions to keep your system safe include budgeting for a security audit, establishing a policy to back up data regularly, and using the proper tools to defend your system.

———. "Hacked!" *American Libraries* 27 (August 1996): 35-36.
This article is the earlier version of the one summarized above. Used in tandem, the two give a very good lesson on what to do to

keep your system from being breached. LaRue suggests to double check identification cards, change passwords frequently, and make sure vendors know who is authorized to deal with them.

Machlis, Sharon. "Hacker Lessons." *Computerworld* 31 (July 21, 1997): 49-50.

Former hackers turned consultants are the premise for this article. One former hacker remarks that many companies spend too much time on perimeter security and not enough on internal system security. Encryption helps, but many times desktop computers are the ones that are compromised.

———. "Hacker Tools Can Give IS a Boost." *Computerworld* 31 (July 21, 1997): 6.

Every network technician or manager should know about the tools described in this article. The best-known network auditing tool is Security Administrator Tool for Analyzing Networks (appropriately called SATAN). SATAN is a UNIX software that is a popular hacking tool, but when used by network managers, it can shut down easy-to-find security holes before a hacker finds them. Several other hacker's tools are also discussed.

McCollum, Kelly and Jeffrey R. Young. "Hackers Attack Thousands of Computers on at Least Twenty-five U.S. Campuses." *Chronicle of Higher Education* 44 (March 13, 1998): A33.

During the first week in March 1998, hackers used the Internet to gain entry into thousands of computers at twenty-five universities across the country. Although no critical information was lost, the attacks were annoying and unusually widespread. The incident affected PCs operating on Windows 95 or Windows NT and connected to the Internet between 7:00 P.M. and 11:00 P.M. on Monday, March 2. To stage the attack, the hackers used a program that sent specifically designed bits of data to a target computer.

Muir, Scott. "After the Break-In Occurs: How to Handle the Student Hacker." *Library Hi Tech* 15 (1997): 92-95.

The University of Alabama is home to 19,000 students, five libraries, two million volumes of books, and an online catalog, VTLS. Muir explains the break-in that occurred when a hacker bypassed the preventive security measures of the computer running the integrated library management system and accessed the operating system. Since the break-in, the library has changed to NOTIS, which has demanded additional security because the NOTIS system shares an IBM 3090 with all other university administrative functions, including payroll and student records.

"No Charges in Hacking Case." *American Libraries* 27 (May 1996): 24.

At about the same time the Ramsey County (Georgia) Library System's computers were broken into, King County (Georgia) Library System's computers were also hacked. Even though there is speculation that the same person did both, it was decided not to prosecute the fifteen-year-old hacker. Instead, the youngster had to complete a series of counseling sessions and perform community service hours.

Pipkin, Donald L. *Halting the Hackers: A Practical Guide to Computer Security.* Upper Saddle River, NJ: Prentice-Hall, 1997. 193pp.

This is a fun, interesting book. Not only is it full of valuable information, it is also well formatted and easy to use. In addition, it comes with a CD-ROM that contains web hotlinks to computer security organizations, mailing lists for the latest information about security breaches, lists of newsgroups, and a potpourri of UNIX security tools such as COPS, SOCKS, and Drawbridge. Pipkin has gathered research from all over and compiled it into this handy sourcebook. What do you want to know about hacking? Anything and everything is right here. One of the more interesting sections is the one in which the author writes with a dual viewpoint — he's both a potential hacker, looking and waiting to break into your system, and he's a system manager, threatened and violated.

Rosachi, Jim. "Give Yourself a Break, Don't Give the Hackers One." *Library Hi Tech* 15 (1997): 99-102.

Noticing an unintelligible message coming through the library computers, the system manager at Sonoma County Library in Santa Rosa, California, immediately checked into the breach and found that an unwanted guest had found his way into their system. During the time of the break-in, all data was lost, a problem that took months to rectify. Working with the local police, the library finally obtained a court order to monitor all incoming calls. At last the culprit was identified and convicted. Rosachi stresses the importance of documenting all intrusions and conducting daily file-saves.

Schuyler, Michael. "Hackers and Hecklers: Protecting Systems on All Fronts." *Computers in Libraries* 18 (March 1998): 30-32.

As system librarian at Kitsop Regional Library System in Bremerton, Washington, Schuyler has the responsibility of making sure his library's computers are secure. However, now that many libraries are putting open jacks in the buildings, computer security is no longer simply a system matter when threats come through the Internet. Instead, the threats are coming from within the building. Even though libraries may not have public access ports, many are using computers at their workstations. Schuyler's remedy to this is to remove the hard drives and hide the disk drives with plastic covers.

Sterling, Bruce. *The Hacker Crackdown: Law and Disorder on the Electronic Frontier.* New York: Bantam Books, 1992. 328pp.

When this book was written, it was considered an entertaining history of hackers. Although there is even more history that should be added to it, it is still an entertaining book about cruising through computer networks, causing havoc.

5. PREMISE SECURITY

As the number of workplace crimes increases, the demand for more secure facilities rises. Most libraries need to be open and accessible to the public; however, they still have a duty to be secure. Building security doesn't only have to do with secure devices or surveillance systems. It also focuses on building design, building placement, and landscaping. As found in the literature, too often there is discord among the architect, the building designer, and the building security officer. Two of them are concerned with the aesthetics and creating a workable space; the third is concerned with the security and safety of the occupants, the equipment, and, as in the case of libraries, the collection. However, by working together and collaborating on both the design and the security of the premises, an end result acceptable to everyone can be achieved.

The Design

When designing buildings with premise security as a consideration, architects are faced with three challenges:

- Determining what is needed, what the purpose of the building is, who the occupants will be, and what the security needs are
- Deciding on the kind of technology needed, what security systems are available for that technology, and what type of security system is being considered
- Making sure the design integrates the appropriate security for the building's purpose (Atlas, 1997)

More recently, some architects and design specialists have begun to use Crime Prevention through Environmental Design (CPTED), to ensure the compatibility of the building design with the security concerns. CPTED can be applied in any building project. As with many new concepts, there are some commonly used strategies:

- The space should be defined by a border of some kind.
- The space needs to have transition zones so users know when they have crossed from public to private areas.
- Hidden cameras or other artificial surveillance measures are effective, but natural surveillance measures, such as windows, open doors, and clear lines of sight can be equally as effective.
- Commons areas should be located where there is good natural surveillance.
- Consider where activities are placed, and make sure unsafe activities are placed where there is natural surveillance.
- Consider placing activities vulnerable to undesirable behavior in easily observable areas.
- Consider what activities are placed near one another. For example, the children's section probably shouldn't be located next to the reading or listening rooms.
- Think about how the space may be scheduled, as in open forum rooms, study rooms, and conference/meeting rooms.
- Adequate communication lines can help in overcoming distance and isolation. Library stacks often stretch to remote areas of the building, as do some quiet study rooms (Crowe, 1991).

Regardless of what design theory or concept is used, there are several practical tips that should be followed:

- Avoid awkward room shapes.
- Avoid dead-end passages.
- Signage should give clear directions.
- Proper lighting is necessary in all areas.
- Protect the book drop against fire or bombing.
- Limit access to areas that process new acquisitions (Martin, 1992).

Once the building designs are completed, the security system, if not incorporated as part of the initial design process, will need to be retrofitted. This is usually the case in remodelings and renovations. During the past ten years, several dozen libraries have undergone major renovations. Renovations cause problems not associated with new-building projects. Primarily, most libraries find that they have to remain open during the renovations. Unlatched doors, plywood windows, and inadvertently turned-off circuit breakers are only a few of the issues libraries in remodeling projects face (Farmer, 1997).

When beginning a renovation, take the time to thoroughly review the building. Thoroughly look at all areas — stacks, corridors, awkward corners, study and reading rooms, rest rooms, staff work areas, microtext rooms, the entrances, and the exits. What lighting should be improved? Is there a good line of sight to the entrance and the exit? Where are the telephones (Martin, 1992)?

Security Systems

Even though security has been built into the building design, it is still necessary to provide security for the collection. The more common security methods are alarm-gates, cameras, and the use of guards or other personnel.

Let's first look at the use of security guards, the oldest method of providing security. Some libraries contract out to security firms, while others use student guards, volunteers, or employ their own employees. There are both advantages and disadvantages to all of these classifications. Some academic libraries have found that the use of student security guards is more effective and very cost efficient. However, student security-force programs must be well structured, have goals for training, and have specific assignments (Huntsberry, 1992).

Other libraries have found that contracting with a security firm provides the kind of protection needed, but high turnover of security staff is a drawback (Winters, 1994). Another drawback is the higher cost of contracting this service out. An alternative to the contractual relationship is the outright hiring of security monitors or guards. Occasionally, the cost is the same, but the library has more control over its own employees (Schindler, 1978). It is vitally important that staff security monitors are well trained. Too often, library staff are called to carry out security functions for which they are unprepared. This has the potential to result in a larger problem.

Although a few libraries still use security guards to check book bags and briefcases of patrons exiting the building, most use some form of mechanical or electronic security system. Theft detection systems have been in use for more than thirty-five years. However, since those first systems were marketed, the technology has changed dramatically. Some systems use electromagnetic technology; others use radio frequency.

In addition to theft detection systems, cameras and/or videotaping at entrances and exits and in other areas of high security concern is being used. The use of surveillance-type systems provides a record of what occurred, but, in the case of material theft, it doesn't alert staff that library materials have been taken from the premises.

Theft detection systems are not without costs. In fact, the decision to purchase such a system usually comes down to dollars and cents (Bahr, 1981). A cost-benefit analysis is an excellent way to be sure the system is worth the price. By looking at equipment, maintenance, and labor expenses, and the time span being considered, compared with the materials replacement amount, it is possible to get an idea of the cost effectiveness of the equipment being considered (Foster, 1996).

One security system not yet mentioned is the metal detector. Why use a metal detector? Why not use one? Airports have them, courthouses have them, the Library of Congress has them. Isn't this a twist on the usual library security system? Generally, librarians don't worry about what is brought in. Instead, librarians are primarily concerned that nothing is taken out that shouldn't be taken out. However, the other side of library security is the safety of staff and users. To better protect staff and users, a security system that checks bags and persons upon entry of a building might be considered (Shuman, 1996).

Building design and security detection systems and methods are all part of securing the area that houses library materials and staff. None can be overlooked in importance. There is a wealth of information on these topics. The following citations are a selective, representative sample of the literature that discusses building security.

Citations

Building Design and Renovation Projects

Atlas, Randall L. "Designing Crime-Free Environments: Making Our Buildings Safer." *Library Administration and Management* 11 (Spring 1997): 88-93.

The demand for more secure facilities is becoming greater as the number of workplace crimes rises. A building must allow efficient job performance, meet the needs of the user, and protect the user from safety hazards and criminal acts. Too often, there is a conflict between the architect and the security officer. One wants openness, while the other wants to be able to control access to the building. Atlas covers several aspects of building design that need to be considered when designing a new building or remodeling an existing one. Nearly every question or issue that might arise when planning a building project is covered.

— — —. "Need for Involving Security in Building Planning and Remodeling." *Campus Security Report* (June 1992): 21.

As vice president of Atlas Safety and Security Design, Inc., Randall Atlas has established himself as an expert in the world of security design. This short, one-page article gives a succinct report on the importance and the problems of using design experts.

Barreneche, Raul A. "Government Building Security." *Architecture* 85 (January 1996): 111-113.

There is a general trend that government buildings need to appear open and accessible to the public; however, security is a must. By careful planning and integration of subtle architectural devices, the risk of occupant injury and property damage from terrorist attacks can be lessened. Different buildings have different security requirements. Regardless of the type of building, the amount and kind of security installed should take into consideration the potential risk to the building and its use. Barreneche also states that it is important to consider the locations of parking lots and the landscaping design.

Cooper, Walter and Robert DeGrazio. "Building Security: An Architect's Guide." *Progressive Architecture* 76 (March 1995): 78-81.

To many architects, building security isn't solely about the type of security system that is installed. It is also about the type of building and the ground or area it is on. Architects need to consider what needs to be secured, where the building is located, and what type of building it is. To make the designing process easier, security should be considered at the start. Quite often, aesthetics plays an important role in the security design.

Crowe, Timothy D. *Crime Prevention through Environmental Design: Applications of Architectural Design and Space Management Concepts.* Boston: Butterworth-Heinemann, 1991.

Crime Prevention through Environmental Design (CPTED) is based on three assumptions: designation of the space, definition of the space, and design of the space. Crowe expounds on the nine most-used CPTED strategies: provide a clear border definition of controlled space, provide clearly marked transitional zones that indicate movement from public to semi-public to private space, relocate gathering areas to locations with natural surveillance and access control, place safe activities in unsafe locations in order to bring along the natural surveillance of the activities, which increases the perception of safety for normal users, place unsafe activities in safe spots, redesign the use of space to provide natural barriers between conflicting activities, improve the scheduling of space to allow for effective use and appropriate critical intensity, redesign space to incorporate more areas of natural surveillance, and overcome distance and isolation through improved communications and design efficiencies.

Farmer, James. "Northern Exposure and other New Building Security Stories." *Colorado Libraries* 24 (Spring 1997): 22-26.

As coordinator of access services and security officer at Colorado State University Libraries, the author is both well versed and has firsthand knowledge of the challenges a renovation can contribute to a library's security. Farmer's article is a compilation of tales the Colorado State University Libraries experienced while remaining open during a major addition and renovation. With unlatched and unlocked doors, plywood windows, and a tenuous entrance and exit, the library saw a wide variety of security snafus. Suggestions on how to handle security issues associated with a building remodeling project are given in an entertaining, authoritative style.

Faulkner-Brown, Harry. "The Role of Architecture and Design in a Security Strategy." In *Security and Crime Prevention in Libraries* by Michael Chaney and Alan MacDougal. Aldershot, England: Ashgate, 1992. 70-87.

Interesting, isn't it, that the architects who build libraries never have to work in them? Therefore, the architect has to rely on the information given and should try his or her best to understand the various library functions. Too often, the architect and the librarian don't see eye to eye. Faulkner-Brown concludes by giving eight examples of careful cooperation between architects and librarians in United Kingdom libraries built between 1963 and 1982. Some points that are illustrated show the relationship between the entrances and considerations given to closets and rest rooms.

Jones, Plummer Alston Jr. and Phillip K. Barton. "Creating Library Interiors: Planning and Design Considerations." *North Carolina Libraries* 55 (Summer 1997): 65-71.

Acoustical treatment, ceilings, clocks, drinking fountains, exhibit space, lighting, public address systems, security (fire and smoke detection), windows, and wiring are only some of the topics covered. When renovating or building a library, it is important to consider the interior from both a security and an Americans with Disabilities Act (ADA) viewpoint.

Libengood, Ronald S. "The Key to Good Security: Proprietary Keyways and Electronic Locks." *Focus on Security* 2 (April 1995): 6-16.

This article takes a different slant on security in that it looks at the use of keys and locks, something most of us take for granted. Some advice that the author gives is to limit the number of doors requiring keys, use a locked key cabinet for control, issue keys only under signatures of the individual and the supervisor, review the record of keys weekly, stamp "Do Not Duplicate" on the keys, and stock replacement locks and cores to allow the replacing of a lock within an hour. Different key and keyless-entry systems are discussed, and illustrations of various kinds of keys are shown.

Lyon, Nina N. and Warren Graham. "Library Security: One Solution," *North Carolina Libraries* 49 (Spring 1991): 21-23.

The authors use the premise that most public libraries are alike, but some have taken the increasing concern of library security to heart. Presented is a case study of the Charlotte and Mecklenburg County Public Library and the steps it took to improve its security during the renovation and addition project of the main library. Included is one page of rules and regulations for conduct in the county public libraries.

MacLachlan, Rachel. "Safety and Security Considerations." In *Preconference Institute on Library Buildings, Equipment, and the ADA.* Chicago: American Library Association, 1996. n.p.

This article examines building requirements as they relate to the disabled and pays particular attention to safety or security concerns.

Martin, Murray. "The Physical Plant: What Are Library Building Concerns?" In *Is Your Library an Accessory To Crime?* Chicago:

American Library Association Buildings and Equipment Section Committee, 1992. 2.

Martin's two-page handout is an invaluable tip sheet filled with pointers to consider when undergoing a building project. He covers designing a new building, retro fitting an existing building, and equipment and signage.

Michaels, Andrea Arthur. "Enhance Security with Effective Interior Planning and Design." *Focus on Security* 4 (July 1997): 7-17.

As access to materials becomes more important to researchers, libraries are finding they need to reassess their building security. Michaels takes a no-nonsense look at library building security and poses dozens of questions for library administration to ask themselves and answer in order to ensure the safety of their collection, staff, and users. She remarks that the bottom line is that libraries can no longer afford to be reactive; instead, they have to be proactive.

Shuman, Bruce A. "Designing Personal Safety into Library Buildings." *American Libraries* 27 (August 1996): 37-39.

Written by the editor of *Library and Archival Security,* this article takes a cursory look at the personal safety of library staff. Shuman notes that there is a trade-off between fulfilling a library's mission and protecting staff and patrons. To ensure more protection for staff and patrons, the locations of furniture and lighting should be considered. A security policy also needs to be in place and understood by all staff members. Security equipment such as alarms and surveillance cameras should also be investigated.

Security Systems

Bahr, Alice Harrison. *Book Theft and Library Security Systems, 1978-1979.* White Plains, NY: Knowledge Industry Publications, 1978. 128pp.

Anyone interested in library security issues must read this book. Yes, this publication is more than twenty years old, and yes, it is dated, but it is a classic. If historic information isn't what you want but you do want to go back thirty, forty, fifty years, Bahr's bibliography, located at the end of the book, does just that. Although most cites are from the 1970s, there are still a representative sample of articles from the 1940s, 1950s, and 1960s. Bahr covers high school, college and university security systems.

— — —. "Electronic Security for Books." *Library Trends* 33 (Summer 1984): 29-38.

Bahr looks at effectiveness, cost, and how security systems work. Do you really need one? Will it be worth the cost? These and other questions are answered in this informative and authoritative article.

Bommer, Michael and Bernard Ford. "A Cost Benefit Analysis for Determining the Value of an Electronic Security System." *College & Research Libraries* 35 (July 1974): 270-279.

This article is included simply because it gives a thorough look at a cost-benefit analysis. The figures are too old to be of use in today's decision making, but the formula is timeless.

Clegg, Susan, Philippa Dolphin, and Jean Sykes. "Security in Academic Libraries." *Library Association Record* 91 (February 1989): 93-96.

The safety of materials and people in British libraries takes its clue from the pro-active measures found in the United States. Using literature about academic library security published in the United States, the authors look at the hardware used in protecting books (3M and Tattletape); how to protect equipment such as televisions, VCRs, and CDs; guidelines for keeping staff safe; and what the future holds. There aren't any new concepts presented, but those that are given are proven and should serve as reminders that library security measures need not be high tech to be effective.

Foster, Cathy. "Determining Losses in Academic Libraries and the Benefits of Theft Detection Systems." *Journal of Librarianship and Information Science* 28 (June 1996): 93-104.

This article reports on a study that determines the accuracy of the statistical sampling techniques used to verify the number of books missing from library collections, as compared to taking a full inventory. The statistical sampling methods were found to be as accurate as the full-inventory method.

Huber, Ed. "Intrusion Alarm Systems in Selected Southeastern Academic Libraries." *Southeastern Librarian* 38 (Winter 1986): 147-150.

Huber sampled 267 academic libraries scattered through the southeastern United States and discovered that 21% of the respondents reported thefts of materials in the two preceding years and that only 19% of these had installed alarm systems.

Huntsberry, J.S. "Student Library Security Patrol: A Viable Alternative." *Conservation Administration News* 49 (1992): 24-27.

The use of students trained as library security agents is advocated. However, it is imperative that the students are properly trained, given specific duties, and assigned to specific schedules. When these variables are in place, students are a very effective and efficient deterrent to theft of library materials.

Knight, N.H. "Library Security Systems Come of Age." *American Libraries* 9 (April 1978): 229-232.

This article is an excellent source for historical information on security systems. All things considered, though, today's technology isn't much different from the first security systems used in the mid-1960s. The brand names described are 3M, Gaylord, Knogo, and Sentronic.

Kollasch, Matthew. "Let's Get Physical." *Wilson Library Bulletin* 67 (September 1992): 69-72.

Trying to curtail material theft, a school library changed its floor plan, installed a security system, restricted its use to school hours, and made a photocopier available.

Leslie, Donald S. "Self-Checkout Systems: Combining Convenience and Security for Libraries in the '90s." *Library & Archival Security* 12 (1994): 63-71.

The advent of self-checkout systems has been a positive time-saver for circulation staff; however, it has brought about different issues in security. Leslie examines the 3M SelfCheck System, the mechanics of its operation, and the built-in security features and how they benefit libraries.

Llewellyn, Brian H. *Standards for Electronic Tagging*. London: Book Industry Communication, 1995. 31pp.

Unfortunately, this book's format makes it a bit difficult to read. In fact, it doesn't have what could be called textual content. Instead, it is more of a detailed outline. Once you are past the formatting of the material, the information is instructive and offers excellent pointers. There are six chapters: security tagging; electromagnetic systems; radio frequency systems and acoustic magnetic systems; the use of security tagging in the book industry; current problems; and standards and their implementation.

Nicely, Chris. "Evaluating Library Security Problems and Solutions." *Public Libraries* 32 (May/June 1993): 154-156.

There are several different types of security systems that libraries can install. This article examines some of these systems and explains the differences among radio frequency, electromagnetic, and microwave technologies.

Roberts, Matt. "Guards, Turnstiles, Electronic Devices, and the Illusion of Security." *College & Research Libraries* 29 (July 1968): 259-275.

This article reports the results of a four-year study of book theft at Washington University's Olin Library in St. Louis, Missouri. It was determined that the theft of library materials was the result of a highly competitive academic environment.

Saulmon, Sharon A. "Book Security System Use and Costs in Southwest Public Libraries." *Library & Archival Security* 8 (Fall/Winter 1988): 25-35.

Keeping collections secure is an ongoing concern for all libraries. This article looks at the prevalence and associated costs of book security systems. Using data from twenty-four southwestern public libraries, a study determined that 100% of the respondents sensitized reference and nonfiction items, 95% sensitized fiction items, 68% sensitized audiovisual materials and periodicals, and only 50% sensitized paperbacks. Some of the recommendations noted in the study included the need to do a cost analysis to compare all costs, such as cash outlay and staff time.

Schefrin, Rita A. "The Barriers To and Barriers Of Library Security." *Wilson Library Bulletin* 45 (May 1971): 870-878.

Schefrin has written a complete review of the literature on library theft prevention and gives the results of a survey she conducted of commercial alarm systems.

Scherdin, Mary Jane. "The Halo Effect: Psychological Deterrence of Electronic Security Systems." *Information Technology and Libraries* 5 (1986): 232-235.

Scherdin's article reports on the effect of installing an electronic theft detection system at the University of Wisconsin-Whitewater's library had on the loss rate of materials. Even though not all materials were sensitized, the psychological effect of the electronic system was enough of a deterrent to cut the number of thefts.

Schindler, Pat. "The Use of Security Guards in Libraries." *Library Security Newsletter* 2 (Summer 1978): 1-6.

As vice president of Stanley Smith Security, Inc., Schindler is an expert on the use of security guards. This article offers practical advice on selecting, training, and supervising guards.

Schonfield, L. and J. Sullivan. "A New Window for Special Collections: Digitizing Photographs and Signatures in a Reader Registration Database." *Computers in Libraries* 14 (1994): 10-11.

The Huntington Public Library in San Marino, California, requires patron signatures and photographs to be stored in a database. Also included are the patron's checkout privileges, professional address, and other pertinent information. The costs associated with the setup and maintenance of the database are balanced by the decrease in theft of materials.

Sheridan, Leslie W. "People in Libraries as Security Agents." *Library & Archival Security* 3 (Spring 1980): 57-61.

Generally, the security of collections depends on mechanical devices, but nearly everyone who works in a library is involved in security of the collection, the staff, and the patrons. However, one of the primary concerns of using staff as security agents is the lack of training. Sheridan takes an unbiased look at using people as security agents and concludes that mechanical devices coupled with trained personnel are vitally important to the security of a library.

Smith, Frederick E. "Door Checkers: An Unacceptable Security Alternative." *Library & Archival Security* 7 (Spring 1985): 7-13.

Westminster College in New Wilmington, Pennsylvania, compared the effectiveness of guards and electronic security systems. The guards were found to be not as effective, and student security personnel were even less efficient.

"Source Security Tagging of Books; Split to Spoil Standard?" *Library Association Record* 98 (January 1996): 17.

This short article reports on a pilot program of source-tagging books. It was shown that printers and binders are able to source-tag books successfully; yet it was also shown that some security equipment in bookstores and libraries is ineffective. Recommended in the report is the use of electromagnetic technology instead of radio frequency technology.

Vincent, Ida. "Electronic Security Systems in Libraries: Measuring the Costs and Benefits." *Australian Library Journal* 27 (September 1978): 231-236.

Vincent examines the costs involved in implementing an electronic security system. Is it worth the price?

Winters, Sharon A. "A Proactive Approach to Building Security." *Public Libraries* 33 (September/October 1994): 251-256.

This article takes a look at the security program the Hampton (Virginia) Public Library put into effect after they moved into a larger facility and noticed that library usage had increased. As Winters mentions, many of the security issues were routine, such as loud children and people eating and drinking. To counteract these complaints, the library contracted with a security firm. However, due to the high guard turnover and the inability of library personnel to convey adequately to the guards what their needs were, the security firm was terminated. Instead, the library hired their own staff to act as security monitors. These monitors not only patrolled the library and quieted noisy patrons, they also assisted users in locating materials and services. The monitors all possessed self-confidence, sensitivity, and strong reasoning skills. In general, only 10% of those who applied were accepted. Backgrounds of the monitors varied and included a former middle school teacher, college students, a probation officer, and a young mother. It was found that the monitor costs were the same as the commercial security guard service but the benefits were far greater.

Witt, Thomas B. "The Use of Electronic Book Theft Detection Systems in Libraries." *Journal of Interlibrary Loan* 6 (1996): 45-60.

No electronic book security system is foolproof, and in order to provide the necessary protection for books and people, a total security program should be implemented. Witt discusses the pros and cons of electronic theft systems.

6. DISASTER PLANS

Throughout the literature that has been referenced in the preceding pages is one common theme: libraries must have disaster
plans. Disasters and accidents happen and, in nearly all cases,
without warning. Through farsighted planning and publicizing the
procedures, serious damage can be avoided. Quite often, disaster
plans amount to evacuating people, while collections and equipment are neglected.

A good disaster plan considers all areas and not only contains
contingency plans, but also contains environmental control, fire
and water damage prevention, and security relating to theft, natural
disasters, chemical spills, and bomb threats. Some disaster plans
even include insurance and risk management information. Within
the plan, response, reaction, and recovery should be discussed
(Borchardt, 1988). When considering the impact of disasters, disaster prevention is less costly than disaster recovery (Buchanan,
1988).

Disaster planning varies from library to library. The size and
type of collection, the building, the staff, and the financial situation
all influence the type of disaster plan that is written. When starting
to draft a plan, advice from different professionals should be
sought:

- librarians or archivists who have experienced disasters
- conservationists who have experience in collections like
  yours
- insurance adjusters and risk managers
- fire marshals
- architects who are familiar with the building
- custodial and facilities staff who know the building and can
  advise on switches and cutoffs (Fortson, 1992)

Disaster plans frequently are written by a committee, rather
than by one person. It's not necessary, but it is helpful, to have a

conservationist or the library's preservation librarian on the committee. All collections, including special collections and archives, electronic labs and software, and alternative format materials, should be included in the plan,

There are several tasks a disaster manual or plan should outline:

- list who is responsible for what duties
- list the phone numbers for the fire and police departments and library administration
- list the locations of power switches
- give the location of insurance policies
- provide documentation for recovery after an emergency (Boss, 1984)

In addition to having a formal, written plan, another aspect of disaster preparedness is the education and training of staff. When a disaster strikes, it shouldn't be expected that staff stop to consult the disaster plan in order to know what to do. It would, therefore, be helpful to have a training session for all staff on what to do when a particular disaster occurs (Fortson, 1992). Security personnel, environmental health professionals, and the library's preservation/conservation librarian should be used to give an in-service training for library staff. Different techniques can be used, including slides, videos, role-playing, and discussion groups.

As we have found from the literature, disasters affect libraries all over the world. The citations below are selective and were chosen because they offer a broad perspective of disaster planning and preparedness.

Citations

Alegbeleye, Bunmi. *Disaster Control Planning for Libraries, Archives and Electronic Data Processing Centres in Africa.* Ibadan, Oyo State, Nigeria: Options Book and Information Services, 1993. 107pp.

This book is the result of research conducted in 1986 on the state of disaster control planning in Nigerian university libraries. Because most of the libraries had no disaster plans, but were eager to draft some, the author wrote this book as a guide to assist them in learning more about disaster planning.

Alire, Camila A. "And on the 8th Day. . .Managing During the First Week of Library Disaster Recovery." *Colorado Libraries.* 24 (Fall 1998): 10-11.

This article is a dean's point-of-view following a natural disaster than destroyed more than 450,000 volumes and an entire floor of a university library. Alire ends with ten lessons learned from the disaster.

Anderson, H. and J. McIntyre. *Planning Manual for Disaster Control in Scottish Libraries and Record Offices.* Edinburgh, Scotland: National Library of Scotland, 1985. n.p.

Although this publication focuses on Scotland, it has a listing of resources available in the United Kingdom. This item is a well-organized disaster planning manual.

Ashman, John. *Disaster Planning for Library and Information Services.* London: ASLIB, 1995. 51pp.

Currently conservation officer at Glasgow University Library, Ashman is well respected in the United Kingdom for his knowledge and expertise on conservation issues. This manual is a practical guide that covers different issues in disaster prevention including preparedness, salvaging water-damaged materials, and conservation of materials. Flowcharts of print and non-print material salvaging are included.

Barton, John P. and Johanna G. Wellheiser, eds. *An Ounce of Prevention: A Handbook on Disaster Contingency Planning for Archives, Libraries and Record Centres.* Toronto, Canada: Toronto Area Archivists Group Education Foundation, 1985. 192pp.

Contingency planning for disasters is an open-ended project. This book covers all the aspects of disaster contingency planning and makes the task less daunting than it appears. Environmental control, fire and water-damage prevention, security, and insurance are discussed. In addition to some text discussion, the authors also include a lengthy bibliography and resource lists of professionals in the disaster field. A word of caution: because this book is almost fifteen years old, the validity of the resources can't be relied on.

Borchardt, Max William. *Disaster in Libraries.* Camberwell, Australia: CAVAL, 1988. 64pp.

Prevention, insurance, response, reaction, and recovery are all covered. This publication is based on the *Scottish Planning Manual for Disaster Control in Scottish Libraries and Record Offices.* The author notes that the text has been modified from the original. Even though this is based on a Scottish publication, disasters happen everywhere. The value of this book isn't necessarily in what it covers, but in how the material is presented.

Brady, Eileen E. and John F. Guido. "When Is a Disaster Not a Disaster?" *Library & Archival Security* 8 (1988): 11-23.
University and, in particular, library catastrophes are not unusual. This article takes a look at the 1985 Washington State University run-in with broken water pipes. With a few thousand water-soaked volumes, the library knew it had to do something to salvage them. Food service freezers were used to start the preservation process of the water-logged materials. The authors relate their experiences in freeze-drying water-damaged materials. In addition to learning about the art and science of freeze-drying as a preservation tool, the library also learned about the importance of disaster preparedness.

Brooks, Constance. *Disaster Preparedness.* Washington, DC: Association of Research Libraries, 1993. 197pp.
Brooks takes the stance that many library disasters could have been prevented had the library been better prepared. To help with disaster preparedness, she has written this resource guide to show how libraries should plan for the worst. She includes twenty-three articles on disaster preparedness to illustrate her claims. This publication is also an ERIC document, ED360999.

Buchanan, Sally. *Disaster Planning: Preparedness and Recovery for Libraries and Archives.* Paris, France: General Information Programme and UNISIST, 1988. 187pp.
This publication was written with two parts in mind: disaster preparedness and disaster recovery. The disaster preparedness section looks at prevention and protection. Prevention is a less costly method than disaster recovery. Recovery looks at both the response to a disaster and the techniques to employ when collections are damaged. Most of the information is dated, even though this publication has a 1988 copyright. The bibliography is primarily sources from the 1970s and early 1980s. Nonetheless, there are enough supporting materials, such as the guidelines for analyzing needs of damaged materials.

— — —. "Disaster Preparedness." *Wilson Library Bulletin* 68 (December 1993): 59-62.

Floods, earthquakes, fires, and vandalism have hit library collections hard during the past few years. Although some disasters strike with no warning, others can be diverted by having a disaster plan in place. However, good disaster plans depend on good communication links. All library staff need to know what to do in the event a disaster strikes. Yet disaster preparedness doesn't stop with a plan. It is equally important to know what insurance limits are set forth in your policy and what items are covered.

Colorado Preservation Alliance. "Disaster Recovery Resource List." *Colorado Libraries.* 24 (Fall 1998): 31-35.

This is an excellent list of Internet resources, national companies and organizations, and Denver area resources for disaster recovery, and is a nice complement to those listed at the end of this book in chapter eight.

Disaster Planning and Recovery: A SLA Information Kit. Washington, DC: Special Libraries Association, 1989. 185pp.

This volume is a reprint from a Scarecrow Press publication of 1983, *Library and Archives Conservation: 1980's and Beyond,* by George Martin Cunha and Dorothy Grant Cunha. What were, at the time, state-of-the-art techniques, are now rather passé and not at all sufficient. We've come a long way, and this publication is proof of that. To illustrate, take a look at the Solinet-reproduced article on spores and the pages on computer disaster planning.

Doig, Judith. *Disaster Recovery for Archives, Libraries and Records Management Systems in Australia and New Zealand.* Wagga Wagga, New South Wales: Centre for Information Studies, Charles Sturt University, 1997. 157pp.

This manual covers the history of disaster recovery and identifies disasters that have occurred in Australia and New Zealand. The author recognizes that management issues need to be considered when recovering from a disaster. Disaster recovery can be very expensive, and even though there may be insurance proceeds, emergency funds should also be requested. There are very good tips on preparing a disaster plan and on training staff to deal with a disaster.

Donnelly, Helene. "Disaster Planning: A Wider Approach." *Conservation Administration News* 53 (April 1993): 8-9, 33.

Electronic data recovery seems to be the focus of disaster plans; however, a disaster plan written primarily for the recovery of computer data and equipment is only touching on a small part of the recovery process. A wider approach to disaster planning should be taken in order to safeguard all vital information, both electronic and written.

— — — . "Disaster Planning in the 90's: Getting it Right." *Law Librarian* 23 (March 1992): 21.

Donnelly takes a realistic view of disaster preparedness. One of her most significant points is that librarians need to think before acting when faced with a disaster. In fact, the initial disaster may not result in the actual disaster. For example, a flood that soaks materials may not be as crucial as the bacteria found in the water from the flood and their affects on the materials and the building.

England, Claire and Karen Evans. *Disaster Management for Libraries: Planning and Process.* Ottawa, Canada: Canadian Library Association, 1988. 207pp.

This publication isn't a slick, professionally printed one, but the information contained within the pages is worth reading. All libraries need to have disaster plans. England and Evans cover every facet of disaster preparedness from anticipating, reacting to, and the preserving of the collection. The authors include an extensive bibliography and a short index.

Ferguson, Mark P. "Now What Do We Do? Training People to Manage Disasters." *Colorado Libraries* 24 (Fall 1998): 27-30.

Ferguson takes the stance that companies tend to pour hundreds of dollars into disaster planning, but seldom do they consider preparing their staff to handle a disaster. He describes several workshops that focus on staff training. One such workshop has been developed by the National Archives and Records Administration (NARA), an independent federal agency.

Fortson, Judith. *Disaster Planning and Recovery: A How-to-do-it Manual for Librarians and Archivists.* New York: Neal Schuman, 1992. 102pp.

This is a very thorough, practical guidebook for libraries that need to write disaster plans. Fortson covers all aspects of disaster preparedness, including insurance and liability issues. It is important to know what is and what isn't covered under the insurance policy. Review the library's insurance policy periodically, and be familiar with it. Carefully document what has taken place if a disaster occurs.

Genovese, Robert. "A Disaster Preparedness Manual, Part I." *Trends in Law Library Management and Technology* 2 (March 1989): 1, 3.

A disaster plan is a necessity in any library, but the plan must be tailored to the library's individual needs. Consider the kinds of materials housed in the building, where the library is located, and who the patrons are.

George, Susan C. and Cheryl T. Naslund. "Library Disasters: A Learning Experience." *College & Research Libraries News* 47 (April 1986): 251-257.

This article is a first-hand look at the unfortunate luck of having the same disaster strike several times. During a building remodeling, water disasters hit the Kresge Library at Dartmouth College eight separate times. Two years prior to the flooding, the library had established a disaster team that had held several training sessions. When the floodings occurred, the disaster team quickly responded and a second team of staff was then called upon to move the damaged materials from the building. In only a few pages, the authors describe their disaster plan and analyze what went wrong and what needed to be done differently.

Kahn, Miriam B. *Disaster Response and Planning for Libraries.* Chicago: American Library Association, 1998. 144pp.

Kahn, a consultant in preservation and disaster planning, has written a very practical guidebook that describes the four key phases in disaster preparedness: response, recovery, prevention, and planning. She gives detailed case studies to illustrate the points she is making.

Mackler, Mark E. *Disaster Planning in the Law Library: First-Hand Perspectives, First-Hand Realities.* Newton, MA: Legal Information Services, 1992. 20pp.

Mackler cites case studies involving California libraries and their responses to disasters. Collections damaged by fires, earthquakes, and floods are examined. Using these case studies, the author illustrates the importance of disaster preparedness and a disaster plan.

Morentz, James W. "Computerizing Libraries for Emergency Planning." *Special Libraries* 78 (Spring 1987): 100-105.

Libraries generally don't put much time and effort into preparing for emergencies. The author contends that the main reason disaster plans aren't routinely drafted is because the libraries don't realize how easy it is to develop plans. Even though this article is ten years old, the basic premise is still true: all libraries need disaster plans.

Morris, John. *The Library Disaster Preparedness Handbook.* Chicago: American Library Association, 1986. 129pp.

Building security, problem patrons, preservation and conservation, water damage, fire protection, and theft of books and materials are all covered. Although the book isn't all-inclusive, it gives the basics and includes important information about insurance and risk management issues. In addition, two pages are devoted to illustrations of common pests that eat paper and book glue.

Mullin, Christopher G. "Some Ideas about Where to Begin." *PNLA Quarterly* 60 (Spring 1996): 11-12.

Disaster preparedness is usually postponed until it is too late. Mullin presents a step-by-step design to follow when you are considering writing a disaster plan for your library. Some tips include identify possible disasters, produce plans for each major contingency and use them to encourage needed improvements, determine what is needed to implement the plans, and review them regularly.

Myers, J. and D. Bedford, eds. *Disasters: Prevention and Coping. Proceedings of the Conference, May 21-22, 1980.* Stanford, CA: Stanford University Libraries, 1981.

In 1979 the Stanford Meyer Library was hit by a flood that damaged books and the building. This report gives general guidance about what to do in the event a disaster strikes.

Panella, Deborah S. "Disaster Planning." In *Basics of Law Librarianship.* New York: Haworth Press, 1991. 52.

Disaster planning isn't completely about plans and what-ifs. Instead, it also encompasses steps to take to ensure the safety of non-printed materials, such as computer tapes. Panella stresses the importance of backing up online catalogs and shelf lists and storing the backup copies off site.

Peake, Carolyn. "Disaster Planning." *PNLA Quarterly* 60 (Spring 1996): 12.

Peake presents a common-sense reason why disaster planning is important. After recovering from a windstorm prior to Christmas 1995, the Lake Oswego Public Library became aware of the gaps in its present disaster plan.

Peterson, Lance. "Contingency Planning Worksheet." *Colorado Libraries* 24 (Fall 1998): 36.

What do you do before, during, and after a disaster? This one page guide offers suggestions on what steps to take, depending on the stage you are in.

Tregarthen, Jenkin I. *Disaster Planning and Preparedness: An Outline Disaster Control Plan. British Library Information Guide 5*. London: British Library, 1987.

This is an excellent source of disaster plans for United Kingdom libraries. It is thorough, concise, and informative.

Van Sickle, Anne. "Building Woes and Potential Disaster." *PNLA Quarterly* 60 (Spring 1996): 12.

Because it had outgrown its library building, McMinnville's Carnegie Library built a 14,800-square-foot addition. During the building project, it was found that the addition had some major flaws that were potentially devastating to the library collection. Unfortunately, a retrofitting project was necessary, and thirteen years after the addition was built, the library was completely finished. Although water damage was still a concern, the retrofitting provided some protection.

Wallace, Marie. "Disaster Recovery Planning." In *Managing the Private Law Library 1989: Delivering Information Services*. New York: Practicing Law Institute, 1989. 533 pp.

Wallace gives practical advice that should be considered by all librarians when evaluating their disaster preparedness skills. One important point is the next time there is a fire drill, think about whether you know what to do if the fire or other disaster were real. Practice what-if scenarios.

Waters, Pater. *Procedures for the Salvage of Water-Damaged Library Materials*. Washington, DC: Library of Congress, 1979. 30pp.

Using the lessons learned from the 1966 Florence, Italy, flood and numerous other disasters in the United States during the 1970s, this guide explains how to salvage water-damaged materials. Although the material on fungicides is outdated, the rest is still valid.

―――. *Primer on Disaster Preparedness, Management, and Response: Paper-based Materials*. Washington, DC: Library of Congress, 1993. n.p.

This is a compilation of reprints that the Smithsonian Institution, the National Archives and Records Administration, the National Park Service, and the Library of Congress issued on dealing with severe storms, bomb threats, earthquakes, and other disasters.

Wood, Larry. "What Lessons Have We Not Yet Learned About Disasters." *Colorado Libraries* 24 (Fall 1998): 4-6.
Wood's article is a step-by-step approach to disaster planning and recovery. He gives several questions that need to be asked while in the disaster planning stage. This article is full of good advice.

Wright, Gordon H. "Fire! Anguish! Dumb Luck! Or Contingency Planning." *Canadian Library Journal* 36 (October 1979): 254-260.
Wright's article suggests that there are nine requirements for a contingency plan and discusses staff problems, security, and the disaster salvage team's responsibilities.

7. LEGAL LIABILITY

Society has become very litigious, and because libraries are no longer simply repositories for printed materials, they are becoming prey to lawsuits. As can be expected, security concerns breed liability issues. The laws relating to material security fall into two areas: one pertains to the mutilation of materials, and the other makes it a misdemeanor to fail to return library materials (Ladenson, 1977). Most states have statutes protecting library materials from mutilation. Theft of library materials is usually covered under the general provisions of the criminal code; however, that isn't always true because some states have specific laws regarding public records and/or library materials. On the other hand, some states are similar to California and have old statutes that make it a crime for a bookseller to purchase works of literature that bear marks of ownership from a library without making certain the person selling the items has a legal right to do so (Ladenson, 1977). Libraries also have a duty to their patrons to provide a safe atmosphere. They are obligated to exercise reasonable care and guarantee that the premises are free of potentially dangerous conditions (Barsumyan, 1988).

Liability Issues

Let's look at some of the instances where there are specific liabilities. The most obvious is the entrance to the building. Is it free of obstacles and accessible? All publicly supported libraries generally guarantee access to their services and collections to almost anyone. However, once inside, other liability issues arise. The use of surveillance equipment may have the potential of interfering with one's right to privacy, but under tort law, surveillance equipment in a public place isn't an invasion of privacy (Forster v. Manchester, 410 PA 192, 189 A2d 147 1963). Nonetheless, library patrons usually are entitled to privacy regarding the use of library materials, but there are no guarantees that they will be completely free from general security screening (Chenkin v. Bellevue Hospital Center, 479 FSupp. 207).

Problem patrons pose a different type of liability concern, and on rare occasions, they become agitated and potentially harmful to others. The library has a responsibility to keep its patrons safe and secure, but occasionally there are some instances when library employees' actions may be suspect and pose a potential liability issue. In general, an employer is not liable for the criminal acts of an employee (Bintliff, 1984). However, there are instances where a library employee needs to stop a patron from leaving the building when a security alarm sounds. There are several states that have codes allowing library employees to detain persons suspected of stealing materials if the employees act in a reasonable manner (Ladenson, 1977).

Although it has just been stated that a library isn't liable for the actions of its employees or of its patrons, there are instances when it may be liable for actions by an individual who is known to be potentially dangerous if that individual is allowed to enter the building (Bintliff, 1984). Libraries have a duty to supervise their users and their employees. If this duty is not taken seriously or the libraries fail to act in a responsible manner, negligence may be found.

Although librarians and information specialists are seldom held accountable for the information they dispense, there are becoming more incidents of librarian malpractice. Ethics and duty of care are becoming more important in the information brokerage arena.

This has been a very simplistic view of tort law, and by no means have all pertinent liability cases been discussed. The citations that follow are to articles that thoroughly explain many of the legal issues that concern libraries.

Citations

Legal Liability

Allred, Carol B. "Negligence Law for Libraries." *Law Library Journal* 77 (1985): 195-198.

Allred's article covers definitions for classes of people who enter library buildings and cites William Prosser (an authoritative legal expert on torts) and gives a clear, easy-to-understand view of negligence law as it applies to libraries. Allred, however, also points out that before there can be a cause for action for negligence, four elements must exist: 1) there must be a legal duty to protect others from unreasonable risks; 2) this legal duty must be breached by failure to exercise the due care of a reasonable person; 3) the risk-taking conduct must be the legal or proximate cause of the resulting injury; and 4) there must be actual loss or damage to another person. Library negligence generally focuses on the first two elements.

Angoff, Allan. "Library Malpractice Suit: Could It Happen To You?" *American Libraries* 7 (September 1976): 489.

Most librarians do not think about a possible malpractice lawsuit. After all, librarians are service-oriented and are not out to trick anyone. Angoff poses an interesting question in this article and forces librarians to think about the work they do and the answers they give.

Barsumyan, Silva E. "Can Your Client Sue You for Misinformation?" In *Information Ethics Concerns for Librarianship and the Information Industry.* Anne P. Mintz, ed. Jefferson, NC: McFarland, 1990. pp. 32-52.

Barsumyan gives practical advice and suggests that reference librarians might consider adding a preface to their, "May I help you?" This preface would consist of a disclosure statement that reiterates that reference service is just that, a service, and the patron may want to do the research him/herself.

———. "Premises Liability." *New Jersey Libraries* 21 (Spring 1988): 9-12.

The basis of property liability is that the owners of property have an obligation to the welfare of the people who are on their property. Libraries are obliged to exercise reasonable care and are liable for injuries resulting from dangerous conditions they knew about. The library's duties are to provide a periodic inspection of the premises in order to detect potentially dangerous conditions.

Bintliff, Barbara and Al Coco. "Legal Aspects of Library Security." In *Security for Libraries: People, Buildings, Collections.* Marvin Brand, ed. (1984): 83-107.

This article limits itself to the liability from the use of security systems. There are several types of security systems employed in libraries ranging from high-tech ones to those as simple as a guard checking book bags and briefcases. Although rather lengthy, this article is an excellent one to read to find out all there is to know about library security systems and the liability issues associated with the systems.

Brown, Yvette. "From the Reference Desk to the Jail House: Unauthorized Practice of Law and Librarians." *Legal Reference Services Quarterly* 13 (1994): 31-45.

Brown refers to the American Association of Law Librarians' code of ethics that requires librarians to avoid the "authorized practice of law while providing access to legal information." What is the difference between providing access to legal information and offering legal advice? This becomes even more tenuous when one realizes that most law librarians also have a jurisprudence degree.

Cremieux, Ronglin A. "Malpractice: Is the Sky Falling?" *Special Libraries* 87 (Summer 1996): 147-153.

Although malpractice in librarianship is an issue that one needs to be familiar with, it is important to note that librarians certainly are not being sued like medical practitioners are.

Dickinson, Philip D. *Workplace Violence and Employer Liability*. Brentwood, TN: M. Lee Smith Publishers, 1997. 68pp.

Workplace violence is a costly issue, not only in terms of security and safety of employees, but also in terms of lost wages. Using guidelines written by the Occupational Safety and Health Administration (OSHA), Dickinson stresses the employer's duty to provide a safe workplace. He also discusses the California Division of Safety and Health guidelines, as well as security acts from other states. The chapter on background checks covers topics such as the Americans with Disabilities Act (ADA), psychological profiles, credit reports, and job references.

Dragich, Martha J. "Information Malpractice: Some Thoughts on the Potential Liability of Information Professionals." *Information Technology and Libraries* 8 (September 1989): 265-270.

Librarians provide information to patrons, but what happens if that information is incorrect, and what happens if the information printed in the resource is incorrect? Sometimes it is possible to see the entire source and then detect the error; however, online information many times can not be evaluated as a printed source.

Everett, John H. "Independent Information Professionals and the Question of Malpractice Liability." *Online* 13 (1989): 65-70.

This article delves into the possible legal actions that could be taken against information specialists when incorrect information is distributed. Everett takes the same view as Barsumyan and recommends using a disclaimer when answering some questions.

Ferguson, Stuart and John Weckert. "The Librarian's Duty of Care: Emerging Professionalism or a Can of Worms?" *Library Quarterly* 68 (1998): 365-389.

This thorough article looks at the issues surrounding the possibility of librarians and information professionals being sued for malpractice for distributing incorrect information. Accountability and duty of care are discussed. The authors also discuss the liability of using online sources and the possibility of handing out false information retrieved via the Internet.

Gray, John A. "Personal Malpractice Liability of Reference Librarians and Information Brokers." *Journal of Library Administration* 9 (1988): 72-73.

Gray categorizes information specialists into three kinds: special librarians, reference librarians, and freelance information brokers. Whether there is a contractual relationship between the patron and the information specialist depends on the latter's classification.

— — — . "Strict Liability for the Dissemination of Dangerous Information?" *Law Library Journal* 82 (1990): 497-517.

Jeppesen, a publisher of aeronautical information, was sued for providing incorrect information on a chart and resulted in a crash landing into a mountain. In this case, Jeppesen used FAA information but converted it into graphic representations. Gray studies this case and notes that what occurred here is not the same as if a trade journal published information received from a source as it was received. Gray's article gives several issues for librarians and information brokers to be aware of.

Hansen, Fay. "Who Gets Hurt, and How Much Does It Cost?" *Compensation and Benefits Review* 29 (May 5, 1997).

Workplace injuries are numerous and expensive. The average yearly workers' compensation premium has been increasing two to three times more than inflation, and between 1985 and 1993, workers' compensation costs rose 75%. Workplace violence is coupled with repetitive motion injuries (RMIs) and highway accidents as having the highest incidence rates. It's hard to believe, but homicide is the leading cause of occupational injury and deaths. Both the National Institute of Occupational Safety and Health (NIOSH) and OSHA have made recommendations meant to reduce the risk of workplace violence.

Kishel, Gregory F. and Patricia Gunter Kishel. "Safeguarding Your Business: Expert Advice on Protecting Your Company from Fire, Theft, and Other Disasters." *Black Enterprise* 23 (July 1993): 98-102.

Written as an excerpt from the authors' book, *How To Start, Run, and Stay in Business,* this article focuses on different liability issues that businesses encounter. Risk management programs allow businesses to cope with increasing work-related injuries. Insurance coverage is the typical measure organizations take to minimize their risks. The authors review fire, liability, workers' compensation, burglary, and comprehensive insurance policies. This article is informative and is a risk management primer in a nutshell. Even though it doesn't pertain to libraries, per se, libraries are businesses, and liability and insurance issues are the same for them as for other businesses.

Kristl, Carol. "Rape of Teenager Raises Security Issues." *American Libraries* 27 (September 1996): 15-16.

The worth of this short, one column article is that it publicizes possible liability issues that face libraries. While waiting for a ride home after the library had closed, a fifteen-year-old girl was raped. The rape raised questions regarding the library's security policy and liability for patrons as they leave the premises.

Ladenson, Alex. "Library Security and the Law." *College & Research Libraries* 38 (1977): 109-117.

Theft and mutilation of library materials is against the law. However, some states compare the theft of materials to shoplifting. This article gives a historical look at laws surrounding the security of library materials. As one can imagine, there are different degrees of theft and mutilation, and to help illustrate these examples, Ladenson cites pertinent court cases.

Law and the Library. Greensboro, NC: North Carolina Library Association, 1991. 52pp.

Published as part of a series, *North Carolina Libraries,* this publication takes a quick look at legal issues facing libraries. Articles of particular note include sexual harassment, library security, and liability in general. Even though the articles aren't in-depth, they are informative and give brief, introductory looks at security issues.

Levett, John. "Libraries, Information Services, and the Emerging Concept of a Duty of Care." *Australian Library* 41 (1992): 3-13.

A reference librarian is no longer seen as "passive, non-thinking, non-judging, non-evaluating dispense of neutral, value-free information whose origins and the quality lie beyond her purview." Instead, there are some powerful verbs being used to describe a librarian's role. These verbs are now putting more responsibility on librarians for the information they dispense.

Mika, Joseph J. and Bruce A. Shuman. "Legal Issues Affecting Libraries and Librarians: Employment Laws, Liability & Insurance, Contracts, and Problem Patrons." *American Libraries* 19 (January-April 1988). Various pages.

Legal issues normally aren't discussed in library schools, but are a real concern for libraries. This is a series of articles addressing the primary areas emerging as legal concerns in the library world. The articles are succinct and serve as good "primers" for a new administrator.

Mintz, Anne P. "Information Practice and Malpractice." *Library Journal* 110 (1985): 38-43.

Mintz examines the issues confronting information specialists and whether the information they give out is correct or not. Included is an interesting Dun & Bradstreet case where incorrect information was distributed by a teenage student and resulted in an incorrect listing being published in the business information report.

Pendergast, John J. III and William E. Smith. *Legal Issues in Workplace Violence in Rhode Island.* Eau Claire, WI: National Business Institute, 1996. 62pp.

As a complement to a faculty workshop on workplace violence, this manual is also an excellent stand-alone publication that would be instructive whether used as a part of a formal workshop or as a resource manual.

Reams, Bernard D. Jr. and Erwin C. Surrency. *Insuring the Law Library: Fire and Disaster Risk Management.* New York: Glanville Publishers, 1982. 142pp.

Reams and Surrency give pointers to follow to help ensure the safety of a library and its patrons, collection, and building. In addition to reiterating advice on insuring the collection, they also remind the reader to take a good look at how and where materials, such as administrative records, are stored.

Rubin, Renee. *Avoiding Liability Risk: An Attorney's Advice to Library Trustees and Others.* Chicago: University of Chicago Press, 1995. 29pp.

Non-profit entities are finding themselves more embroiled in legal battles than ever before. Rubin's book is a discussion of the various liability issues that face nonprofit boards, such as library friends groups and trustees. Some of the information is not explained in enough detail to be of value, but Rubin does point out that her publication is not all-inclusive.

Samuelson, Pamela. "Liability for Defective Information." In *Computers, Ethics, and Social Values.* Deborah G. Johnson and Helen Nissenbaum, eds. Englewood Cliffs, NJ: Prentice-Hall, 1995. pp. 539-548.

In the past, books and computer software have been treated differently by the courts, and the courts are reluctant to prosecute authors and publishers for incorrect information because it might have a negative effect on the free exchange of information. However, the judicial system is now taking this same stance in relationship to online information.

Segal, Jonathan A. "When Norman Bates and Baby Jane Act out at Work." *HR Magazine* 41 (February 1, 1996): 31-35.

Even though an attorney wrote this article, it cannot be construed as containing legal advice. It does, however, give solid guidance about dealing with employees who engage in disagreements at work. All employees are legally liable for workplace violence. According to OSHA, employers must protect employees from foreseeable violence. Additionally, injured employees cause a rise in workers' compensation claims; therefore, higher insurance premiums result. Segal gives hypothetical situations that cover a variety of workers' compensation incidents.

Shaver, Donna, Nancy S. Hewison, and Leslie W. Wykoff. "Ethics for Online Intermediaries." *Special Libraries* 76 (1985): 238-245.

Too many times librarians tend to give patrons what they think they need to know and not what the patron has asked for. The authors guard against this trait and couple it with the case where a librarian retrieves a full-text list of information resources rather than a short list of citations.

Steele, Thomas. "Law of Premises Liability as Applied to North Carolina Libraries." *North Carolina Libraries* 49 (Spring 1991): 9-12.

Nationwide, injuries from slipping and falling comprise the most frequent injuries in libraries. Most of the falls occur on stairs or in entryways. In addition to these injuries, there are also those that involve third parties and those due to negligence. For injuries to be considered negligent, four elements must be present: 1) a duty on someone's part to protect others from risk; 2) a breach of that duty; 3) a causal connection between the breach and the injury; and 4) actual loss caused by the injury. Libraries are held accountable for liability the same as other businesses. Until the 1960s, charitable institutions, including private libraries, were shielded from liability under the charitable immunity doctrine; however, this no longer holds true. It is important to note that state college and university libraries are not protected by the government immunity doctrine that offers protection to local government libraries.

— — —. "Managing Legal Liability." *Library Administration & Management Journal* 11 (Spring 1997): 94-101.

Legal issues are not unique to libraries, but generally the ones that libraries have been associated with involve copyrights and privacy, not legal liability, as associated with library security and safety. Some of the issues Steele covers include children, violent acts, risk management, and insurance. To conclude, the author states that library management can lessen the possibility of injuries to staff and patrons and lessen the risk and impact of personal injury lawsuits by using good management techniques. Included are sample incident report forms and work request records.

Sykes, Phil. "Liability for Information Provision: Spectre or Reality?" *Aslib Proceedings* 43 (1991): 189-198.

Can librarians be held responsible for giving out information that is only partially true? Sykes takes a look at the possible accountability of a researcher when only part of the requested information is found.

Tryon, Jonathan S. "Premises Liability for Librarians." *Library & Archival Security* 10 (1990): 3-21.

Too often, administrators forget about the liability associated with their building and the fact that hundreds, if not thousands, of patrons walk through their doors daily. What is the tort liability that a library may incur when people are injured while on library property? Tryon spends several paragraphs defining different classes of people: trespassers, licensees, and invitees. A trespasser is anyone who is on the premises without permission or some right to be there. How, you may ask, could a public institution label a library patron as a trespasser? Anyone in the building after-hours and not invited would be a trespasser. In general, trespassers are not afforded rights if injured while on the property. A licensee is someone who is allowed to be on the premises but whose purpose is to his or her benefit only. An example would be someone who uses the library as a shortcut to another building. While older courts held that licensees were to receive the same rights as trespassers, recent courts have said that the landowner must warn the licensee of potential and hidden dangerous conditions. An invitee is a person who enters the premises for his or her benefit and the benefit of the owner. In other words, it is someone who enters to do business. Liability is at its highest when considering invitees. Little by little, though, states are abolishing these categories. Tryon's article is well researched and presents negligence and tort liability in laypersons' terms.

Veitch, Anne and Jane Forrest. "AACOBS Report 1981-1982." *Australian College Libraries* 5 (March 1987): 3-11.

This hard-to-find report gives valuable advice to information professionals and states, " . . . . librarians are to act as guides to sources. If they accede to any requests for specialized advice this should be done with a disclaimer or any skill or knowledge of the subject."

Violence in the Workplace: A Study of Workers' Compensation Claims Caused by Violent Acts, 1991-1995. Salem, OR: Department of Consumer and Business Services, Information Management Division, 1996. 7pp.

This is a more recent statistical finding of workers' compensation claims in Oregon caused by violent acts. Included are statistics on occupational fatalities, disability claims, types of violent acts, and the average claim costs for violent claims. In Oregon, a disability claim is one that involves more than three days of lost work, permanent disability, or in patient hospitalization.

Wan, Ronglin. "Reflection on Malpractice of Reference Librarians." *Public Libraries* 33 (November-December 1994): 305-309.

Wan takes a look at the issue of librarians being held accountable for the information they dispense.

Warner, David. "A Rule Mandating Safety and Health?" *Nation's Business* 85 (September 1997): 28.

A 1995 OSHA draft on safety and health programs calls for businesses to have programs in place for managing safety and health and for identifying and controlling workplace hazards. Pushed by statutes that show "thousands of workers are killed and millions are injured" each year, OSHA is working on getting this draft in place because it is more pro-active than the 1970 Occupational Safety and Health Act.

8. RESOURCES

Theses and Dissertations

Bingham, Curt Allen. *Library Security and Book Theft: Private, Public, and Junior Academic Institutions.* Master's Thesis, Western Illinois University, 1985.

Catanzaro, Jean Melissa. *Violence in the Workplace: Strategies for Preempting Anger and Conflict.* Honors Thesis, University of South Florida, 1995.

Davis, Jeanne A. *Violence in the Workplace: The Impact of Narrow Definitions of Violence on Managerial and Organizational Responsibility.* Master's Thesis, Hamline University, 1996.

Gilsrud, Linda F. *Violence in the Workplace.* Master's Thesis, Mankato State University, 1995.

Johnson, Billy S. *The Effect of Using Automation in Library Administration Upon Loss of Library Materials.* Master's Project, Virginia State University, 1990.

Jurman, Steven Joseph. *Target: Workplace Violence.* Master's Project, San Diego State University, 1995.

Lorenzen, Michael G. *Security Issues of Academic Libraries.* Master's Paper, Ohio University, 1996.

Odle, Charlene. *An Analysis of Conflict Management as it Relates to Family and Workplace Violence in the United States.* Master's Thesis, Central Missouri State University, 1995.

Schwalbe, Elisabeth. *The Growth of Stress in Librarianship: A Content Analysis of the Literature, 1974-1990.* Master's Thesis, University of North Carolina at Chapel Hill, 1991.

Walters, David Craig. *Violence in the Workplace: A Prevention and Intervention Education Guide for Management.* Master's Project, San Diego State University, 1996.

Wright, Gwen. *Violence in the Workplace.* Master's Thesis, Sienna Heights College, 1997.

Zarlenga, Marla M. *A Communication Model for Violence in the Workplace.* Master's Thesis, Cleveland State University, 1995.

Zito, Jacqueline. *Workplace Violence: An Examination of its Relationship to Fairness, Work Relationships, and Work Environments.* Master's Thesis, Fairleigh Dickinson University, 1996.

Videos, Sound Recordings, and Cassettes

Security:

American Association of Law Libraries. *Library Access, Security Issues and Justice for All.* Valencia, CA: Mobiltage, 1995.

Sound cassette of conference given in July 1995 at the American Association of Law Libraries. Covers all issues related to library security.

Be Prepared: Security and Your Library. Towson, MD: American Library Association Video, 1994.

Videotape designed to assist library staff in developing a security program. There are eight parts, each covering a different security issue, such as how to approach problem patrons, law enforcement cooperation, and internal theft.

Controlling the Confrontation: Arch Lustberg on Effective Communication Techniques. Towson, MD: American Library Association Video, 1989.

Narrated by renowned media coach Arch Lustberg, this forty-four minute video offers suggestions on defusing confrontations.

Gaylord Guardian Library Security: A Search for Answers. Syracuse, NY: Gaylord Brothers, 1993.

A seventeen-minute videotape and guidebook on library security methods.

Getting What You Want: How to Reach Agreement & Resolve Conflict Every Time. Baltimore, MD: Library Video Network, 1992.

This video communicates three steps to use when negotiating to ensure reaching an agreement.

Indiana Libraries Video Magazine. Indianapolis, IN: Indiana State Library Video Service Center, 1995.

Videotape that discusses library security measures in different county libraries in Indiana.

Is Your Library an Accessory to Crime? Chicago: American Library Association, 1992.

Two sound cassettes on a panel discussion sponsored by the American Library Association's (ALA) Library Administration and Management Association's Building and Equipment Section, Safety and Security of Library Buildings Committee. Discusses security measures and safeguarding library buildings and the grounds.

Library Security: Exit Controls. Provo, UT: Falcon West Media, 1985.

In fourteen minutes, this videotape discusses different methods of providing security at exits. Also comes with a workbook.

Library Security: Expecting the Unexpected. Provo, UT: Mountain West Library Training, 1987.

Videotape and workbook covering methods to use to increase employee awareness of critical security issues. Also gives basic instruction on what to do when problems arise.

Library Security: Providing a Safe Environment for Staff and Users. Chicago: Teach'em, 1994.

A sound cassette of a program on library security given at the Fifth National Conference of the Public Library Association.

Library Security, Who Cares? London: British Library, National Preservation Office, 1990.

This video focuses on security issues in British libraries.

A Library Survival Guide, Managing the Problem Situation. Baltimore, MD: Library Video Network, 1987.

Describes different problem situations and how to deal with them.

Michalke, George. *Dealing with Security Problems in the Library.* Cleveland, OH: Case Western Reserve University, 1989.

This hour-long video takes a thorough look at a wide variety of library security issues. Has more of a legal focus than other videos.

Pro-active Safety Attitudes: Target Zero. Virginia Beach, VA: Coastal Training Technologies, 1995.

Training video that gives managers information on creating an accident-free workplace. Includes a workbook and a leader guide.

Safeguarding WSU Collections, Our Mutual Responsibility. Pullman, WA: Multimedia Services, Washington State University, 1993.

Steve Huntsberry, the police detective who was instrumental in bringing in Stephan Blumberg, notorious book thief, reports on library and museum security.

Violence and Problem Patrons:

Community Policing I: Responding to Violence in the Workplace. St. Louis, MO: ALERT Partnership, 1996.

Videotape and training guide that include points of view of private security and public law enforcement.

Creating an Effective Employee Discipline Process. Canada: Canada Law Book, 1997.

Video and workbook designed to help human resource managers and supervisors effectively discipline staff without causing more problems.

Defusing the Explosive Customer. Brookfield, WI: National Crisis Prevention Institute, 1995.

Consists of a forty-minute videotape, a guidebook, and a personal prevention plan. Designed to help managers recognize potentially violent conflicts in the workplace.

Domestic Violence, How to Help Victims and Keep Your Workplace Safe. Brookfield, WI: National Crisis Prevention Institute, 1996.

Two videotapes, fifty-four minutes long, and two reference guides. Volume one looks at assessing dangerous situations, and volume two covers development of a safety plan for victims.

Ehrlich, Howard J. *Prejudice and Violence in the American Workplace, 1988-1991.* Ann Arbor, MI: Inter-University Consortium for Political and Social Research, 1993.
A computer disk of a study that examined the nature and extent of prejudice-based mistreatment of employees in the workplace.

Grupe, Robert C. *The Corporate Resource Series.* Oklahoma City, OK: Robert C. Grupe & Associates, 1994, 1995.
Six sound cassettes that discuss topics such as understanding violence in the workplace.

Handling Difficult People. Stockport, England: Executive Business Channel, 1996.
Three videotapes and a ring-binder text. Tape one covers harassment; tape two is on bullying; and tape three is on conflict.

Managing Employee Hostility. Brookfield, WI: National Crisis Prevention Institute, 1995.
A forty-minute videotape and reference guide that present three programs to help managers recognize and defuse potentially violent incidents.

Managing the Problem Library Patron. Goshen, KY: Campus Crime Prevention Program, 1993.
Videotape that gives guidelines on how a staff member can deal with problem library patrons.

Managing the Kids' Behavior in the Library. Memphis, TN: Memphis/Shelby County Public Library and Information Center, 1995.
A videotape of a training session on how to deal with children who exhibit restless and unruly behavior.

Mantell, Michael. *Ticking Bombs: Violence in the Workplace.* Buffalo Grove, IL: CorVisionMedia, Inc., 1995.
A two-part training video based on Mantell's book. Designed for supervisors and management. Gives a step-by-step model for workplace violence prevention.

Preventing Workplace Violence. Atlanta, GA: Georgia Department of Labor, 1995.

A thirty-two-minute video on prevention of violence and employee crimes in the workplace.

Respectful Workplace: Opening the Right Doors. Bellevue, WA: Quality Media Resources, 1994.

Consists of a video and workbook on workplace violence. Also comes in a closed-captioned version.

Responding to Violence at Work. Brookfield, WI: National Crisis Prevention Institute, 1995.

Part of a series called *Street Smart from 9 to 5*, this videotape comes with a guidebook and a personal prevention plan. Illustrates how employees can reduce their chances of being in violent incidents and how to protect yourself if you are assaulted.

The Right Moves, Self-Protection on and off the Job. Shaumburg, IL: Video Publishing House, 1995.

Videotape that gives methods of dealing with threatening situations that might occur in the workplace.

Surviving the Workplace Jungle. Des Moines, IA: Excellence in Training Corporation, 1996.

Videotape that comes with a workbook and facilitator guide. Looks at the physical aspects of a workplace and how they impact potential violent crimes.

Taking Control of Workplace Violence. Minneapolis, MN: Media Productions, Inc., 1995.

A seventeen-minute videotape with a participant workbook and instructor guide. Discusses workplace violence and what staff can do about controlling unacceptable behavior.

Understanding, Preventing & Surviving Workplace Violence. Falmouth, MA: SEAK, Inc., 1994.

Three sources of workplace violence are discussed in this fifty-minute video. Looks at issues from a manager's point of view.

Violence in the Workplace. Washington, DC: United States Chamber of Commerce, 1995.

Part of the *Quality of Learning* series. A videotape of a down-linked seminar that discussed the legal and psychological issues surrounding workplace violence.

Violence in the Workplace. Oakland, CA: Kaiser Foundation Health Plan, 1995.
Videotape focusing on crime occurring in the workplace. Part of the series *Medicine in the Nineties.*

Violence in the Workplace. LaPorte, TX: Safety Short Production, Inc., 1996.
A summary sheet and short, eight-minute video on different types of violence and what to do if you are attacked.

Violence in the Workplace, Reduce the Risk. Santa Monica, CA: Quality Line Enterprises, 1996.
Eighteen-minute videotape discussing measures to reduce and prevent workplace violence.

Violence Prevention in the Public Workplace. St. Paul, MN: Minnesota Satellite Technology, 1997.
Videotape of a satellite conference recorded in September 1997 on the work environment and crime prevention.

Weapons in the Workplace. Brookfield, WI: National Crisis Prevention Institute, 1994.
Videotape that focuses on keeping weapons out of the work environment.

Workplace Violence, Dealing with a National Epidemic. Medford, OR: Educational Systems & Resources, 1997.
Hosted by Jerry Counsil, a familiar face on educational videos, this videotape is in panel-discussion format and contains advice from several different experts in the field of workplace violence.

Workplace Violence: Recognizing and Defusing Aggressive Behavior. Santa Ana, CA: American Training Resources, Inc., 1997.
Designed for supervisors and management, this video points out the warning signs of dysfunctional behavior that can lead to violence. Also gives intervention tips for supervisors to use to approach troubled employees.

Workplace Violence, the Risk from Within: Awareness & Intervention Training. Media Partners Corporation, 1994.

How to recognize violence, what to do to prevent it, and how to defuse a violent situation are all covered in this twenty-four-minute video.

Workplace Violence, What Supervisors Can Do. Washington, DC: American Bankers Association, 1995.

Part of an American Bankers Association series about violence in the workplace, this video focuses on the responsibility of the supervisor in keeping the work environment safe and secure.

Sexual Harassment:

All the Wrong Moves. Boston: Videolearning Resource Group.

Illustrates the do's and don'ts of handling sexual harassment complaints. Twenty minute video.

Employee Awareness: Sexual Harassment. Boston: Videolearning Resource Group.

Thirteen-minute video that gives guidelines for acceptable behavior in the workplace.

Handling the Sexual Harassment Complaint. Boston: Videolearning Resource Group.

Short video that shows how to train managers and supervisors to respond correctly to a sexual harassment complaint.

Proactive Management and Sexual Harassment. Santa Ana, CA: American Training Resources, Inc., 1996.

Designed for supervisors and management, this video presents a proactive approach to preventing sexual harassment and illustrates the importance of anti-harassment policies.

Sexual Harassment: Shades of Gray. Boston: Videolearning Resource Group.

In-depth training video that focuses on resolution and prevention.

Sexual Harassment Quiz. Boston: Videolearning Resource Group.

Uses scenarios to illustrate how to handle complaints of sexual harassment.

Computer Security:

Man the Ramparts, Securing Your System in Cyberspace. Chicago: American Library Association, 1997.

Two sound cassettes of a program sponsored by the Public Library Association's Technology in Libraries Committee and the Library and Information Technology Association's (LITA) Telecommunications Interest Group. Covers computer networks and computer security.

Disaster Planning:

Disaster Planning for Libraries. Austin, TX: Concordia Lutheran College, 1992.

Videotape that discusses the importance of disaster planning and gives tips on implementing a disaster plan.

Library & Archival Disaster Preparedness & Recovery. Oakton, VA: BiblioPrep Films, 1986.

A videotape and workbook covering all facets of library and archival disaster planning.

Conferences and Seminars

Workplace Violence:

American Arbitration Association. *Workplace Violence Approach: A Collaborative Approach.* Newton, MA: American Arbitration Association, 1996. Various pages.

Conference proceedings from the April 18, 1996, conference on workplace violence. Topics include mental health and prevention of employee crimes.

Institute of Business Law. *Crime and Violence in the Pennsylvania Workplace.* Santa Monica, CA: Institute of Business Law, 1995. 461pp.

Conference proceedings of workplace violence conferences held in the fall of 1995 in Philadelphia and Pittsburgh, Pennsylvania. Papers cover all issues of workplace violence.

National Conference on Law and Higher Education. *Seventeenth Annual National Conference on Law and Higher Education.* St. Petersburg, FL: Stetson University College of Law, 1996. n.p.

This conference covered several areas of liability, affirmative action, and workplace violence as they pertain to higher education institutions.

Violence and Social Control in the Home, Workplace, Community, and Institutions. St. John's, Newfoundland: Institute of Social and Economic Research, 1991. 322pp.

This publication contains the papers given at the Institute of Social and Economic Research conference. Has an international focus and covers all issues related to workplace violence.

Violence in the Workplace. Chicago: Defense Research Institute, 1997. Various pages.

This publication contains the information given at an April 10-11, 1997, seminar in New Orleans, Louisiana on workplace violence. Excellent resource for someone putting together a short workshop on workplace violence.

Violence: Liability & Damages. Seattle, WA: Washington State Trial Lawyers Association, 1995. 247pp.

Materials given at the September 21, 1995, legal education seminar on workplace violence. May be too technical, in legal terms, for the layperson, but is thorough and covers the law.

Computer Security:

Computer Security Foundations Workshop. Rockport, MA: IEEE Computer Society, 1997. Various pages.

Compilation of papers given at this Institute of Electrical and Electronics Engineers (IEEE) sponsored workshop. Covers all topics of computer security, including cryptographic protocols, recursive authentication protocols, and SDSI's linked local name spaces.

Fore, Julie A. "System Security: When Enough is not Enough." *IOLS '97, Proceedings of the Twelfth National Conference on Integrated Online Library Systems.* Medford, NJ: Information Today, 1997. 53-62.

Fore's paper stresses the importance of adequate computer and system security in today's electronic library.

World Wide Web Sites

Workplace Violence:

http://204.71.249.80:80/home.htm

Safety Online web site listing publications, live chats, a safety forum, Occupational Safety and Health Administration (OSHA) information, and lots more on safety and security issues.

http://dps.state.mo.us

Missouri Capitol Police web site that contains authoritative information about workplace violence.

http://galaxy.tradewave.com/editors/weiss/WorkSD.html

Assault Prevention Information Network web site on violence at work. Contains hotlinks to books and videos on violence in society and several very good articles.

http://www.amdahl.com/ext/iacp/pslc1.toc.html

Combatting Workplace Violence web site containing guidelines for employers and law enforcement officials, and tips on establishing a program.

http://www.amdahl.com/ext/iacp/pslc.index.html

Private Sector Liaison Committee publications of public safety interest. Lists several public domain publications relating to combatting workplace violence and drugs in the workplace.

http://www.com/m2/swj/

Surviving the Workplace Jungle web site giving tools for developing a self-directed workplace violence prevention program.

http://www.execpc.com/~cpi/

National Crisis Prevention Institute's Violence Prevention Resource Center. Offers training in the management of disruptive and assaultive behavior.

http://www.igc.apc.org/fund/workplace/

Domestic violence in the workplace web site containing lots of interesting information about domestic violence and how it invades the workplace.

http://www.umn.edu/mincava/workviol.htm
Higher Education Center Against Violence and Abuse web site on workplace violence that has several hotlinks to other web sites on violence.

http://www.up.edu.au/safework/whatis.html
Safe College of Workplace health and safety web site. Established in 1990, the site lists occupational heath and safety training courses.

http://www.wt.com.au/~dohswald_pubs/violent.htm
Worksafe Western Australia web site of safety and health issues.

Ergonomics:

http://engr-www.unl.edu/ee/eeshop/rsi.html
University of Nebraska computer-related repetitive strain injury (RSI) web site. Offers links to Internet resources and tips on how to improve your posture at your workstation.

http://ergo.human.cornell.edu
CUErgo web site from New York's Cornell University. Contains a wide variety of information on ergonomics.

http://ergoweb.com
Commercial site that encourages the visitor to subscribe to its services. Regardless, it is still very good and subscribers are able to sign up for an ergonomic evaluation by one of its consultants.

http://library.ucr.edu/~pflowers/ergolib.html
ErgoLib web site. Excellent web site containing tips, articles, discussion groups,and hotlinks to dozens of ergonomic related web sites.

http://www.demon.co.uk/rsi
United Kingdom web site with global links. There is a special link for United States visitors that gives names of doctors specializing in RSIs, ergonomic facts, and statistics.

http://www.hfes.org
   Human Factors & Ergonomics Society web site. Contains society news and information. Also lists upcoming conferences.

http://www.lib.utexas.edu/Pubs/etf/index.html
General Libraries Ergonomic Task Force of the University of
Texas at Austin. Has hotlinks to dozens of pertinent web sites.

http://www.virginia.edu/~enhealth/ergonomics/toc.html
   Web site of University of Virginia that gives quizzes and practical tips on stretching exercises.

Computer Security and Hackers:

http://csrc.ncsl.nist.gov/virus
   National Institute of Standards and Technology (NIST) virus
information web site.

http://kumite.com/myths
   Computer virus myths web site. Very interesting and informative.

http://www.cert.org
   Lists programs that can be used by and against hackers.

http://www.cert.org
   Computer Emergency Response Team (CERT) Coordination
Center web site that gives answers to frequently asked questions
about computer security.

http://www.cis.princeton.edu/sip/java-faq.html
   Java Security: Frequently Asked Questions web site that is full
of information about Internet security.

http://www.cs.princeton.edu/sip/java-ys-activex.html
   Security trade-offs web site of Java versus ActiveX.

http://www.microsoft.com/office/antivirus.asp
   Microsoft Office Anti-virus Information Clinic. Informative
and has virus tools you can download from the site.

http://www.microsoft.com/security
Microsoft Security Advisor. Lists programs, white papers, and product information.

http://www.ncc.co.uk/30it.html
National Computing Centre Limited web site that gives several important tips on information security.

http://www.icsa.net
International Computer Security Association web site. Has hotlinks to a wide variety of information on computer security issues and products. Formerly was the National Computer Security Association.

http://www.ntsecurity.net
Microsoft Windows NT security web site. Contains dozens of hotlinks and information about NT security.

http://www.rstcorp.com/javasecurity/links.html
Java Security Hotlist. Has hotlinks to books, papers, and discussions on security issues. Maintained by Dr. Gary McGraw.

http://www.securityserver.com/cgilocal/ssis.pl/category/@hacker5.htm
Gateway to Information Security. Contains information on security links, computer hacking, and other computer security topics.

Serials

Accident Analysis & Prevention. Tarrytown, NY: Pergamon Press, 1969-.
Bimonthly publication addressing risk analysis, safety engineering, safety management and policy, and occupational safety.

Applied Ergonomics: Human Factors in Technology and Society. Oxford, England: Elsevier Science, 1969-.
Emphasizes human ergonomics and task analysis.

Campus Law Enforcement Journal. Hartford, CT: International Association of Campus Law Enforcement Administrators, 1970-.

This journal takes a practical approach to campus security and crime issues. Practitioners write most of the articles.

Canadian Journal of Criminology. Ottawa, Canada: Canadian Criminal Justice Association, 1958-.
Originally this journal addressed corrections, but has since broadened this focus to include criminology. Excellent for its international coverage.

Ergonomics: An International Journal of Research and Practice in Human Factors and Ergonomics. London: Taylor & Francis, 1957-.
Scholarly publication on research conducted in the ergonomic field. Authored by the International Ergonomics Association and the Ergonomics Society.

Focus on Security. Moscow, ID: Triad Co., 1993-.
Quarterly newsletter covering all aspects of library, archival, and museum security.

International Journal of Occupational Safety and Ergonomics. Greenwich, CT: Ablex Publishing, 1995-.
Quarterly journal that was started out of the 1993 World Conference of the International Ergonomics Association. Workplace safety and ergonomics are covered.

Journal of Interpersonal Violence. Thousand Oaks, CA: Sage Publications, 1986-.
Bimonthly journal that delves into the sociological and psychological bases of violence. Sexual harassment, rape, and aggressive behavior are among the topics covered.

Library & Archival Security. New York: Haworth Press, 1980-
Semi-annual journal publishing articles on all facets of library and archival security. Also gives coverage to international security concerns. Formerly was *Library Security Newsletter,* 1975-1978.

Occupational Hazards: The Magazine of Safety, Health and Environmental Management. Cleveland, OH: Penton Publishing, 1938-.
The American Industrial Hygiene Association's trade journal. Issues discussed include workers' compensation, legal liability, ergonomics, and computers.

Occupational Health & Safety. Waco, TX: Stevens Publishing, 1976-.

Air quality, ergonomics, health management, computer applications, and regulations/standards are covered in this monthly, refereed journal.

Police and Security News. Kulpsville, PA: Days Communications, 1984-.

This trade publication contains up-to-date information about practical security topics. Training, equipment, and security techniques are a few of the issues discussed.

Safety and Health: The International Safety, Health and Environmental Magazine. Itasca, IL: National Safety Council, 1919-.

Monthly journal aimed at keeping the public aware of safety, health, and environmental issues. OSHA, Environmental Protection Agency (EPA), and workers' compensation laws are reviewed.

Safety Science. New York: Elsevier Science, 1976-.

A refereed journal that covers ergonomics and worksite hazards.

Author and Title Index

193

Subject Index

About the Author

Teri R. Switzer received a master's degree in library science in 1973 from the University of Illinois and a master's degree in business administration in 1977 from Colorado State University. She is an associate professor and interim assistant dean at Colorado State University Libraries, Fort Collins, Colorado.